Catrina Davies was born in Snowdonia and grew up around Land's End, Cornwall. She has worked as a DJ, gardener, circus cellist, cleaner, TEFL teacher, dog walker, flower-picker, builder and waitress. She has also released two records. Her first book *The Ribbons are for Fearlessness* is a memoir about busking from Norway to Portugal. *Homesick* is her second book.

Also by Catrina Davies

The Ribbons are for Fearlessness

HOMESICK

Why I Live in a Shed

Catrina Davies

riverrun

First published in Great Britain in 2019
This paperback edition published in 2020 by

riverrun

An imprint of

Quercus Editions Ltd
Carmelite House
50 Victoria Embankment
London EC4Y 0DZ

An Hachette UK company

A CIP catalogue record for this book is available
from the British Library

Paperback 978 1 78747 866 4
Ebook 978 1 78747 864 0

10 9 8 7 6 5 4 3 2 1

Typeset by CC Book Production
Printed and bound in Great Britain by Clays Ltd, Elcograf S.p.A.

MIX
Paper from
responsible sources
FSC® C104740

Papers used by Quercus are from well-managed forests and other responsible sources.

Author's Note

Everything in this book is true to my experience, although some names and details have been changed, and some individual characters are composites of several real-life characters. I have also altered the time-scale in which events took place, sometimes re-ordering the events, and squashing several years into one. I hope the reader will forgive me these liberties. They were designed to protect peoples' identities and to make this a good story, as well as a faithful representation of my life in the shed.

For my mother,
with love and gratitude for giving me a childhood
that was made of more than economics.

'As we degenerate, the contrast between us and our house is more evident.'

Ralph Waldo Emerson

'In Wildness is the preservation of the world.'

Henry David Thoreau – from an address
to the Concord Lyceum in 1851

Contents

Homesick

I am flat on my back in the ocean. It's early enough in the morning for me to be the only person in the world. The sun is rising out of the east, spilling light on my face. The horizon is an invitation. There's a seal nearby. Seals are people-watchers, they like to observe our habits. I kick my legs, flip over and dive under the surface of water, crossing the line between sea and sky. I keep my eyes open and let the salt wash in and out of my open mouth. The sun's rays have crossed the line too. There are infinite shades of blue.

I am on my way home. It feels good to think the word 'home'. I rattled around rootless for years before I finally managed to carve myself a space for living. Not that I've been near it all weekend. Spring dragged me outside into the warmth and lengthening days, night skies crowded with stars and blackbirds singing themselves half to death. It's been a weekend of driftwood fires and Spanish guitars and lying upside down on the surface of the earth.

But now it's Tuesday and there's work to do – the messy and mostly unpaid business of hacking the meaning out of life with words and music. Also, I'm hungry. I swivel to face the horizon one more time, then swim towards the shore. I let a gentle wave deposit me on the cold sand, which is made of billions of billions of tiny pieces of shell. I pull my clothes on without bothering to dry myself first (towels are for pussies). I clamber over the granite boulders and haul myself up to the footpath. The footpath is overrun with honeysuckle. The air smells of nutmeg. There are swallows high up above me, floating and swimming in the sky.

I'm thinking about porridge. I'll make it with milk from the farm. Or maybe I'll get eggs from the stall. Only I can't remember if I've got any bread. Even if I do, it'll probably be mouldy by now. Porridge, then. I'll drink my coffee in the garden, with the sparrows. Then I'll settle down to work at my home-made desk.

I'm drafting and redrafting my second book, which is proving even harder to write than my first book, which was hard enough. The first one was about running away. This one is about coming home, or trying to. It's about how the value of being at home is cancelled out by the soaring cost of having a house. I'm using *Walden*, by Henry David Thoreau, as a lens to help me understand how the current housing crisis sweeping across many parts of the world is a symptom of a deeper homesickness, and how it's also manifesting as crises in ecology, social justice and mental health. I've been exploring the reasons why I felt so homesick when I lived in a house, and yet, now that I live in a shed, I don't feel homesick at all. I'm trying to explain that living in a shed isn't a cop-out, or a bum's choice, or a romantic hippy dream, but my answer to an impossible question: how to balance on an economic system that is fundamentally unsound.

This is what I'm thinking about as I walk up the steep path that leads from the beach to the top of the cliff. My hair is dripping down my back, my feet are bare, my trainers are in my rucksack.

Lots of people have heard of *Walden*, or at least they've heard of Thoreau. They've read that he was the world's first hippy, and that he lived for a time in a wooden cabin on the edge of a pond, extolling the virtues of simplicity, growing beans and making bread, sitting in his doorway for hours on end, watching the birds and silently smiling at his 'incessant good fortune'. Thoreau might have been the world's first hippy, but he was also an activist. His choice to spend two years alone in a wooden cabin was less about running away and more a bold statement about the rampant, blinding materialism of his age, proof that another way of life was possible.

There are plenty of similarities between Thoreau's world and mine. The town he grew up in, Concord, suffered a major economic downturn just after he graduated from Harvard. Most people in Concord didn't own any land, and most of the wealth was concentrated in the hands of just fifty individuals, an inequality that was getting worse, not better. The telegram had just been invented, radically changing the way people communicated with each other, just as the internet has radically changed the way I communicate. Cheap steam presses had led to a proliferation of cheap, partisan newspapers that distorted political discourse – the nineteenth-century version of fake news. There was a growing backlash among young people against what they saw as a fundamentally flawed system. In the words of Robert Sullivan, 'The paths to adulthood were not what they once had been, and the rough and rowdy subculture, the hip-hop generation of its time, was rising.'[1]

Like me, Thoreau split his time between writing and manual labour, sometimes working as a kind of servant to the wealthy poet Ralph Waldo Emerson, helping to look after his children and tend his garden. Thoreau understood that it can be quicker to walk somewhere, even somewhere far away, than to spend the time to earn the money to buy the ticket for the seat on the train.

Thoreau died young, of tuberculosis, but his thoughts are still very much alive. *Walden* was published in 1854, and it's been in print ever since. I love that stories can persist for hundreds of years after their authors have died. *Walden* is as relevant today as it was when it was written. If anything, it's more relevant. In the face of ecological Armageddon, the message to slow down and simplify is urgent.

I pause halfway up the steep path and turn towards the ocean. There are two seals now. I watch them for a while as they rest in the morning sunlight, doglike heads bobbing peacefully. A flock of gulls whirls and chants its way to the sea. The seals dive under the water and disappear. I continue my climb to the top of the cliff and turn inland towards a row of big houses. Most of the houses are not lived in; they are rented out during the holidays at extortionate prices to people who are exhausted from toiling in the city, people who dream of seals and waves and freedom. I can't help dreaming about living in one of these empty houses, watching the sun rise out of the sea every morning, having a room for sleeping and a different one for eating and another one for working, digging up the lawn and growing flowers and vegetables in the garden.

The big houses throw their shadows over the path. A man is loading bags into the back of his car. I catch his eye. The holiday is over. I stop feeling envious and remember how lucky I am. In a world full of wars and prisons and torture and poverty and call centres and endless miles of traffic jams, I have everything I need. Most importantly, I have time. The only thing I don't have is money. I pull my bike out of the hedge where I placed it for safekeeping and freewheel home, singing.

I love coming round the bend on my bike in the early morning and catching sight of my sea-coloured shed, nestling comfortably on its crossroads, the sparrows lined up on the roof as if they're waiting for me. My shed is an old corrugated-iron structure, eighteen feet by six, in a fairly advanced state of disrepair, but I have worn it down with love and made it shine. I have mingled my particles with the old wooden walls, and made it mine.

My keys are stashed in a secret compartment in the little Berlingo van my boatbuilder friend sold me, which is parked in front of the shed. I lean my bike against the van, open the compartment and take out the keys. I go to unlock the door and I know, with a flash of animal instinct, that something is wrong.

The first thing I notice is that the chair has moved. Charlie must have let herself in to charge up her phone. Charlie lives in a shed, too, only her shed still has no electricity. But why did she leave the chair facing the wall like that, and why are all those empty boxes on the bed, and where are all my things?

Where are my hard drives?

Where is my precious collection of forty-fives?

Where is my laptop?

Everywhere I look, something is missing. My microphones, mixer and sound cards, my box of cables and the loop pedal I bought second-hand for fifty pounds. My tools and drills and puncture repair kit. My guitar case and Logic disks, my camera, my penknife, my handheld recorder, all the SD cards. The only things left are my books and my clothes, my cello (thank Christ – it must have been too heavy in its battered plywood case) and my collection of warped and stringless guitars. I frantically try to remember when I last emailed myself a copy of the manuscript I've been working on for the best part of three years. I have a hollow feeling it was months ago.

The back door is swinging open. I wander, gasping with shock, into the garden. My sweet-pea seedlings, which I nursed into being from wrinkled brown seeds, have been trampled. I can hear myself making noises like an animal caught in a snare. My pickaxe is lying on the floor by the outside tap. Slowly, the truth is dawning on me. Someone broke my door with my pickaxe and took all my things. Questions ricochet around my head. How did they know that I had a pickaxe, and that it was leaning against the hedge in the apex of the tiny triangle, hidden under the buddleia that I planted for the bees and the butterflies? How did they know my heavy pickaxe would be just right for breaking the lock on the glass door the boatbuilder made, forcing it open and breaking the glass? How did they know the door was crafted out of reclaimed materials that were slowly cracking and warping with time and rain and wind?

My shed is not defined like houses are. The edges are blurred. My kitchen is outside, for example. My living room is outside, too, in the spring and summer and autumn. Winter storms blow in through the thin walls and rickety doors. The locks are rusty and don't always hold, because the doors are made of wood that expands and contracts depending on the moisture in the air.

They must have been watching me for weeks, planning how they would park their car up the lane, climb over the gate into the field, then into the allotments and into my tiny triangular garden, breaking the rotting wooden fence in two places. I imagine them laughing at how easy it was to break into my shed and take away all the things I paid for with my life: waiting, serving, cleaning holiday cottages, tidying other people's gardens. I try to laugh at how hard it will be for them to sell my things, how little they will get for their trouble. My life is not worth very much, in monetary terms. I know this because, sometimes, when it's winter and I'm particularly skint, or desperate for an adventure, or both, I try to sell bits of it on eBay. I'm not laughing. I remember I had a hundred pounds in cash, the folded notes hidden in a small wooden box covered in patterned blue silk that Dad gave me on my eighth birthday. I check the shelf where the box lives, but the box is gone. I reel out of the front door and into the road. I'm still making noises like an animal caught in a snare. There's a woman on a bicycle. She stops and asks if I'm okay, then she calls the police.

The policewoman closes her small black notebook and pushes it into her breast pocket.

'Do you have household insurance?'

I shake my head. 'It's not a house.' No insurance, no insulation.

'But you live here, don't you?'

'Yes,' I reply, and I feel sick.

This is not nineteenth-century Massachusetts, however much I want it to be. This is twenty-first-century England. There are planning laws. I am not supposed to live in a shed. The policewoman might tell the council. It has happened before, more than once. Somebody lodges an anonymous complaint and I receive an official letter from the planning enforcement officer:

ALLEGED UNAUTHORIZED RESIDENTIAL OCCUPATION
OF SHED: JUNCTION OF MAIN ROAD (CROSSROADS)

I live in permanent dread of these letters.

The policewoman's radio crackles into life. Someone has fallen off the cliffs at Land's End. It's an emergency. The policewoman tells me to make a list of everything that's missing, and says someone from forensics will come and check for fingerprints. I sit cross-legged on the floorboards, numb and silent with shock, trying to see what isn't there, noticing more and more things. Dad's old levelling instrument with the receipt dated 1948, my printer, my phone charger, my bike lock. The worst part is knowing they were in here, in my shed, in my home, rummaging around in my things, moving my chair, sitting on my bed, breaking my fence. I feel violated and unsafe. My van was there, parked in the space between the shed and the metal signs with the black and white chevrons. How did they know I was out? What if I *hadn't* been out?

I don't want to touch anything. There's a footprint – it's on the wooden decking that I made myself out of scaffold planks that were being thrown away from a building site where my friend, Chris, was working. The man from forensics carefully copies the print on to a piece of clear plastic, using a special sort of dust. There are no fingerprints. The thieves were professionals. They wore gloves.

When the man from forensics has left, I sit on the edge of the bed and stare at the familiar wooden walls and wooden ceiling.

My shed is far from the ideal home, and it lacks basic comforts like hot water, but it's my home and having it means I get to live life on my terms. Even when I'm skint, I don't feel poor. Sometimes I feel cold and grumpy and resentful and restless with cabin fever, but mostly I feel like I've dodged a bullet. The alternative to living in the shed is slavery, or so it seems to me. Indentured to somebody else's mortgage.

The opposite of slavery is freedom, not idleness, and freedom is what my shed represents. Freedom to work, and work hard, on things that matter to me. Freedom to be paid badly to do things well. Freedom to refuse to do bad things just because they pay well.

But everything has a price, and the price of freedom is security.

The neighbours come, one by one, to tell me they are shocked and sorry. The son of the old fisherman who died reaches out and hugs me over the broken fence. The hug is awkward and reassuring. I lie on my back on the decking made of scaffold boards and pallets. The sun has dissolved into rain. The rain is soft and warm. The weather is kind, at least. The field behind the allotments, which once belonged to a poet, is full of ghosts and emptiness.

I go inside. My skin is cold and clammy. My thoughts are confused. I'm tired. I want to go to sleep. But I can't sleep in my shed anymore, not with the door swinging open and shadows in the field.

If only I had written my book with a pencil, like Thoreau

would have done. I try not to think about the folders full of notes and research, the clippings and quotes and thoughts and sentences and paragraphs that are gone forever. Maybe this is the universe trying to tell me the book is no good and I should just let it go. Maybe this is the universe trying to tell me my life in the shed is not viable. It occurs to me that it might be a relief not to try to write books anymore.

My boyfriend, who is younger than me and doesn't have a shed, rents a bedsit in a concrete barn on the other side of the peninsula. I go to him and he holds me when I wake up in the middle of the night, crying. I lean against the cold concrete wall and weep for my book and my photographs and all the videos and songs and stories I had recorded and organized and saved, and all the things it took me years to get the money together for to buy. But most of all I weep because my shed is broken and I feel like I can't go home.

The weeks that follow are a blur. I drive the length and breadth of Cornwall, looking for my things in car-boot sales and auction houses, cash convertors, pawn brokers and second-hand shops. I change all my passwords and panic that I didn't do it soon enough. I search my email for a draft of the manuscript and my stomach turns over when I see how old it is, how much is lost. I save the draft on to a borrowed laptop and try to forget about it, but three weeks later, when I've given up looking for my things and I'm wondering how to pick up the pieces of my life, the boatbuilder calls and asks if I need a place to work. I go to his house and establish a makeshift desk in his studio. It's where he stores his things when he rents his cottage out and moves into his van. The boatbuilder's cottage is in a terrace that climbs vertically up a steep hill. I can see acres of crooked roofs, with hundreds of seagulls guarding their particular chimneys. I can see the seagulls croaking, but I can't hear them, because of the double glazing. I can see the tops of the trees swinging in the wind, but I can't hear the wind. I watch the seagulls for a long time before I finally force myself to open the file. It feels like peering at starlight through a telescope, going back through time and space to a world that has already died.

Why I Live in a Shed

The mass of men lead lives of quiet desperation.*

When I wrote the following pages, or rather the bulk of them, I lived alone on the edge of a crossroads, in a shed made of wood and corrugated iron, three miles from the nearest shop and a mile from the ocean, with a handful of buildings to the north and east and nothing but fields and sky to the south and west.

The buildings were a mixture of old granite cottages built several hundred years ago for the village blacksmith and the men who worked on the farms, square pebble-dash houses built much later for their children and grandchildren, and, in the gardens of what used to be a vinery, terraces of tiny concrete bungalows. Some of the bungalows were rented out to locals and some were rented out to gangs of farm labourers from other parts of Europe, where the value of the pound compared to their local currency made labouring on British farms economically viable. The rest seemed to be rented out to an ever-changing rota of people who got on the train at Paddington and fell asleep until Penzance and then walked west as far as the road went, searching for a place to rent. They would stay for a while, and then move on, or, more likely, out, into a tent or a hedge or a cave. In the seven years since I first slept in the shed, rural homelessness had been rising steadily, although it was less obvious than in the towns. There was a period when I was woken often at night by the sound of footsteps on the crossroads. My brother-in-law gave me a broken air rifle, which I kept propped by the door until gradually the fear subsided and I forgot that the sense of safety my shed provided was mostly symbolic and you could knock it down with a hammer in an afternoon.

Most of the fields around my shed belonged to a lord who lived in a castle on an island. Many of the lord's farmhouses had been converted into holiday homes, while most of his fields were worked for profit by tenant farmers. Judging by their grim expressions and the size of their tractors and the speed at which they drove them back and forth along the narrow lanes, the tenant farmers worked hard. In fact, the farmers worked so hard, scientists were having sleepless nights. There were less than a hundred harvests left, they warned, before the soil was dead. The fields that belonged to the lord looked brown and sad and exhausted. But they turned a profit, and that was the main thing.

There was one field that wasn't farmed intensively. This field belonged to a poet and it supported all sorts of things that weren't profitable, like foxgloves and thorns and thistles and nettles and hogweed and mallow and bedstraw and countless other forms of life whose names I still don't know. The poet's field was popular with bees and buzzards and a pair of barn owls who needed this kind of rough, unsprayed grassland because it harboured the field voles they relied on for their survival.

Beyond the wet woodland were cliffs, and the cliffs were criss-crossed with paths, although most of the paths were made by rabbits or ponies or cows and few people apart from me ever walked on them. The paths led to a series of bays which were inaccessible to humans and therefore loved by seals. The seals spent their days basking on the rocks and fishing in the sea and giving birth to pups that sometimes washed up on the more accessible beaches after violent autumn storms. The bays were divided by ragged headlands, where gulls and fulmars, crows and choughs, ravens, buzzards and kestrels took advantage of the wind to swoop and swirl and fly in circles.

You had to walk right to the edge of the cliffs to understand this time-worn landscape. You had to stand on the very edge of the cliffs and turn to face the land to see that the cliffs were in fact the unbreakable souls of tall mountains that had been scrubbed and flattened by 270 million years of time. These ancient cliffs were the heartrock of my place, and, like the innermost heartwood of an ancient tree, they kept all sorts of secrets.

From the top of the cliffs, the ocean was a flat blue carpet that stretched from land to infinity, translucent as the sky. But if you clambered down to sea level and paddled half a mile out towards the horizon on a surfboard or a kayak, it revealed itself to be dark and deep and full of mysterious limbless creatures that lived in underwater forests where the bones of drunken sailors rotted with the remains of their wrecked boats, and burgeoning lakes of plastic gathered in the currents like shoals of fish.

Opposite my shed was a pond. The pond was home to an assortment of ducks and geese that liked to play chicken with the cars. From my vantage point on the corner of the crossroads, I could see cars coming from both directions. I'd watch in horror as the ducks led their tiny ducklings into the path of oncoming traffic, and in admiration when the geese lay down in the middle of the road and refused to move. The geese succeeded in bringing to a halt, not only cars, but open-topped double-decker buses overflowing with visitors, combine harvesters with their blades glinting in the sunlight, and juggernauts brimming with potatoes destined to be thinly sliced and fried in oil and sold in plastic bags as crisps. The geese had thick necks and violent eyes, muscular wings and a ferocious hiss, and they behaved like pissed-up rioting members of UKIP. I enjoyed leaning over the bottom part of my stable door and watching the cars and lorries stack up behind the geese, the drivers honking their horns and trying to contain their rage, then getting out and attempting to chase the geese out of the road. The geese were having none of it. They would rise up and chase the drivers back into their cars, flapping their wings and hissing. Then they would lie right back down in the middle of the road.

If you found the pond by accident, you probably wouldn't even notice my shed. You'd be busy coping with the ninety-degree bend and trying not to squash the geese and the ducks and considering whether to buy quails' eggs (how strange!) or strawberries from a sort of wooden cupboard, which you saw a moment too late, jamming on the brakes and reversing dangerously towards the blind corner, wondering what the hell you were doing. But then, when you'd got your tiny speckled eggs and were buckling yourself back into your warm and comfortable seat, you might notice that you were parked a few metres from a crossroads and that there were two single-track lanes going off in different directions, one south and one west. And you wouldn't be able to help wondering what was at the end of them, but you'd decide not to drive down, in case you couldn't turn around and come back. There was a signpost, but it had rusted through and the sign had broken off and all that remained was a post.

If you did notice my shed, you might assume it had self-seeded and grown out of the ground like a wild apple tree, rather than being planted seventy years ago by a pair of twins who liked to carve birds out of pieces of wood. It held on impressively for such a flimsy structure. It had held on through half a hundred storms, including the hurricane of 1987, which lifted greenhouses clean out of people's gardens and deposited them in a thousand pieces several miles away. I put the survival of my shed down to its tree-like qualities, which allowed it to bend with the wind rather than standing firm and cracking under the pressure of resistance.

I was aware that from the outside my life in the shed

probably seemed bizarre and desperate, especially at the start, when the building was a derelict eyesore that looked like it was about to fall down. But from the inside it was a lot less desperate than my previous lives had been, in tents and caravans on other people's land, or renting rooms in houses that cost the earth. I liked the light and the solitude, and I liked spending most of my time outside, adjusting my behaviour to the strength of the wind or the depth of the cold, like the sparrows who hid in the spiky blackthorn and came out singing with the sunshine. I swapped fridges and radiators for freedom, and although my lifestyle had its challenges, I came to believe that freedom was worth any amount of material deprivation.

Which is not to say that I didn't talk often and at length about the virtues of a hot shower. Doing without is the best way to ensure a good yield of pleasure from even the most mundane things. I never went to visit a friend without taking a towel and a spare pair of knickers.

Economy

The cost of a thing is the amount of what I will
call life which is required to be exchanged for it,
either immediately or in the long run.

Before I wrote the following pages, or any pages, I rented a room in a house in Bristol, which I shared with four other adults and a child. Before that, I lived with my ex-boyfriend in a static caravan, just outside the town where I went to secondary school. Before that, I lived in a yellow Iveco van. Before that, I lived for two months in a room in a cottage near my primary school, while the person who actually lived in the cottage was on holiday. Before that, I lived in a room in a house near the static caravan. Before that, I lived in a tent outside the backpackers' hostel where I worked as a waitress, because the person I was renting a room from before *that* suddenly got a new girlfriend and kicked me out.

The house in Bristol belonged to a family who were travelling the world on our combined rent. From their perspective, this probably seemed like a perfectly reasonable thing to do. They were maximizing their assets in order to get the very most out of their lives. From my perspective, it was upsetting, not least because they had put the house in the care of a letting agent, and the letting agent had his own key. He used his key to spy on us, and these regular intrusions were legal. Because my room was technically a box room and not a bedroom, and this was written into the tenancy agreement (which did not include me), I had to eradicate all traces of my existence in preparation for these inspections. Eradicating myself was so annoying, I fell into the habit of staying permanently eradicated. The walls were bare. I kept my books in old plastic daffodil crates I had used for moving since my days as a flower picker for Winchester Growers. I didn't unfold the sofa bed, but slept on it folded. It gave me a bad back. My room had one window, which looked straight out on to a red brick wall.

Rent was a monthly trauma. My housemates and I argued a lot over bills. My thirtieth birthday came and went, then my thirty-first. I'd busked my way through life, hawking a bizarre and random set of skills that ranged from circus bands and cello lessons to writing for websites and DJ'ing in clubs and bars. I had moved to Bristol because I dreamed of building a life out of books and songs, but, now that I was there, everything was slipping from my grasp. I couldn't think straight in the box room. I sang in the bathroom with the taps running, so my housemates wouldn't hear me. I couldn't hear me either. I was so busy with all my random jobs, I didn't have the energy to even think about writing a memoir about busking from Norway to Portugal, which was, at that time, the project that haunted me. Instead I obsessed about housing.

I read articles online about how the only people who could do things like write books and record songs were people who could live with their parents until the books and songs could pay the rent. My parents struggled to house themselves. There was no way they could house me.

It was dark in the box room. I sat up on the bed and reached for the light switch. I turned on my old MacBook. It had holes in the white plastic casing where the battery had expanded, but more often than not it worked. While the internet was buffering, I felt panic-stricken. I had read plenty of self-help books. I knew I had to harness the law of attraction to get what I wanted. I had to stop generating all this negativity. I had to visualize what I wanted, instead of dwelling on what I didn't want, and what I feared would happen.

I wanted to watch something meaningless and stupid to distract myself from my thoughts, but the laptop refused to connect to the internet. I turned it off and got into bed. I was hungry, but I couldn't face the kitchen. I couldn't face my housemates. Some of them were friends and some were strangers. Some of the ones who had been friends weren't friends anymore, which seemed to be what happened when you tried to live with four other adults and a child, in a house that had one kitchen and one bathroom and lots of shared utility bills. I was crap at sharing. I hid in my room. Eventually I fell asleep. I woke up the next morning to the sound of people shouting at each other in the kitchen.

I lay with my eyes closed, trying to hang on to a dream about surfing. I was standing at the top of a steep cliff, holding my surfboard. There were perfect waves breaking at the bottom of the cliff and I was desperate to get to them, but I couldn't find a way down. There were other people in the water, and they were waving at me to join them, but I couldn't work out how they had made it to the base of the steep cliffs, because there was no path.

The shouting in the kitchen turned into the sound of plates being smashed. It reminded me of the parts of my childhood I wanted to forget. The house was full of tension. It seemed like everyone was about to snap.

I pulled the duvet over my head and imagined I was walking to the edge of the sea. The sea in my mind was very cold and very clean. I imagined wading in, dipping my head under the surface, letting the water rinse the inside of my mouth and eyes, tasting salt and plankton, feeling salt gather on the end of my eyelashes, so that, when I turned around, the land was blurred. The longing for salt water on my skin and the sound of gulls crying and the unfolding horizon of a sea dawn felt like a deep thirst. I was parched. I could have drunk the whole wide ocean, if it hadn't been so far away.

I emerged from under the duvet and opened my eyes and stared at the cracks in the plastered ceiling. The washing machine was going into its spin cycle. It sounded like an aeroplane taking off. I reached for my phone. Seven thirty. I sat up and swung my legs on to the floor and rested with my elbows digging into the tops of my thighs and my head in my hands. I remembered the £400 a month, plus bills, and how this meant I was entitled to go into the kitchen and make myself a coffee, even when my housemates were throwing plates at each other.

There were pieces of antique dresser all over the kitchen floor. The dresser belonged to the family who owned the house, who had our deposits. 'Morning,' I muttered, finding a path through the broken glass to the cooker. I unscrewed my stove-top espresso maker, which was the one I had bought when I moved into the yellow Iveco van. I filled the little perforated tray with coffee from my tin. I put water in the bottom part, screwed it back together and put it on the stove. I heard my housemates leave the room. I tried to relax my shoulders. I went to the fridge to collect the small plastic carton of milk I had bought the previous day on my way back from teaching cello to someone who worked in computers. He had rung me after the lesson to tell me he had decided he was too busy to learn to play the cello and wouldn't be needing my services anymore. Losing him as a client meant I would have to find another way of making up the rent – and quickly. The milk carton wasn't in the fridge. It was next to the cooker with the lid off. It was empty. I took a cup of black coffee back to my room. I turned on my laptop and stared at the screen, waiting for it to light up.

I knew I was one of the luckiest people on the planet. I wasn't one of the 65 million forced out of their homes by war or famine or persecution. I wasn't one of the 28 million refugees and asylum seekers hoping for sanctuary in hostile countries like mine. I wasn't one of the many millions so thoroughly hounded out of their homes that they were officially stateless.[2] I wasn't waking up on the side of the street in a cardboard box, like the several hundred thousand people with the exact same passport as me. Not yet, anyway. My life probably wouldn't be over at forty-three, which was the average life expectancy of a homeless woman in Britain.[3] I was safe and warm and educated. I had no right to feel so miserable. My childhood had been chaotic and sad at times, but I'd had plenty of advantages and I'd always been loved.

I was born in a terraced cottage near a slate quarry in a remote valley on the fringes of Snowdonia, close to where both my parents grew up. We moved over the mountain when I was two, to a smallholding with goats and chickens. When I was five, we left Wales for Land's End, in Cornwall. We lived there until my parents couldn't afford the mortgage and then we moved to a nearby valley, where my parents rented a tiny cottage from the National Trust. We moved three more times before I left for university, by which point my parents were divorced. I spent the holidays in a tent in the garden of the flat Mum was renting, or stayed in college and paid for my board by cleaning the rooms of my fellow students. After university, I wandered around Europe on my own. I did my best to pretend I was a Zen monk practising non-attachment. In truth, I was lonely and homesick and scared. Dad eventually managed to get himself into social housing, but Mum kept on moving. Tenants' rights had been eroded so much, her rent kept going up with no warning (there was no limit on how much it could go up), or the houses she rented would be sold while she was living in them and she would be given two months' notice to find somewhere else.

By the time I moved into the house in Bristol, I was in my early thirties. I was heartsick for my ex and the static caravan, even though I was the one who broke us up. I did it mainly because I couldn't stand sharing a static caravan. Sharing a static caravan is not conducive to a happy and harmonious relationship. 'Water is important to people who don't have it,' wrote Joan Didion, 'and the same is true of control.'[4]

I was desperate to live on my own. I wandered the streets of Bristol, picking out apartments. I dreamed of living by the river. In my imagination, I converted abandoned buildings, old water towers and warehouses, garages and workshops. I went to the boatyard and gazed at the narrowboats. There was a whole block of empty flats, designed to look like a ship. They had been built before the 2008 crash, and now the developer was having trouble selling them. I chose a small one, with a view of the water. It had two rooms and a tiny balcony. There was space for me and my books, my record players and my guitars. It didn't matter that I had no furniture. I would sleep on the floor. I would cook on my tiny camping stove. The important thing was that I would make the rules, and I would stay until I wanted to leave.

The problem was money. I was skint. I was always skint, and the older I got, the more I couldn't imagine ever not being skint. Being skint was a headache, a constant pressure on my skull. Being skint meant small mistakes quickly became big problems. There was no room for error. Being skint meant doing things I didn't want to do and not doing things I did want to do. Being skint meant living my life on other people's terms.

I had not always been skint. When I was twelve, I inherited some money from my grandad on Mum's side. He was from a working-class background, bright but poorly educated. His influence on Mum's life was very negative and he left her nothing when he died. At the age of twelve, I didn't understand the value of money. All I knew was that my parents worried about it a lot, and that worrying about money was making Mum ill. Mum and Dad's relationship was collapsing. Dad spent more time in the pub than at home. I was desperate for my parents to be happy. What I wanted was for them to stay together and for everything to be all right. They did not stay together and everything was not all right.

I used some of the money I inherited to buy a cello, because my parents wanted me to have one and couldn't afford to buy it. I used some of it to pay for driving lessons when I turned seventeen. I used far too much of it to buy a second-hand Ford Fiesta from a dealer. I lived on it when I broke my arm and couldn't work. It was all gone by the time I got to university. Lacking any sort of financial education, I squandered my inheritance, the only one I'll ever have, before I even knew what it was worth.

My little sister was as clueless as I was, but my big sister was smart. She saved her money and put it towards buying a flat. Ten years later, she sold the flat for ten times what she'd paid for it and, together with her husband, who'd also inherited money, she bought a house that needed lots of work. She and her husband did the work. My sister has three children. Every summer, they all move into a tent, all five of them and the dog, while the house is rented out to strangers. This is hard, but not unusual. People I know with houses squeeze every drop of capital out of them, because, even when it's hard, squeezing capital out of a house is a hell of a lot easier than squeezing it out of work.

Housing is a casino. If I was a little bit older, or a little bit wiser, I could have been on the other side of this gulf, a whole different person with a whole different life and totally different opinions, lolling around on the property ladder, home and safe and dry. But, by the time I knew what I needed, the stakes had changed completely. What everyone liked to call the 'housing ladder' was about three miles up in the air and I had next to no chance of even catching hold of it, let alone hauling myself on to the bottom rung.

Average house prices had grown about seven times faster than the average income of young people since I turned eighteen.[5] When I left university, a deposit to buy a starter home in the UK was about nine months' average salary. Ten years later, it was three years' average salary, and rising.[6] If food prices had risen as fast as house prices in the years since I came of age, a chicken would cost £51[7] (or £100 for those living in London[8]).

I was taught that if I worked hard and lived an honest and generous life then I would be rewarded. This was misguided. I should have been taught to grab hold of that ladder and stamp on the hands of the people below me.

According to my massive dictionary (not the concise, but the *physically compressed* OED), which has so many words crammed into it you have to use a magnifying glass to catch their sense, the word 'rent' has two meanings. The first, from the Old French 'rente' or 'rendre', means paying or receiving regular payments in exchange for the use of land or property. The second, from the Old English 'rendan', means to pull asunder or in pieces: to tear one's face, hair or clothes in grief or rage.

Living in Bristol, trying to keep up with the rent and not get into actual fights with my housemates, I felt like I was being pulled asunder. There was a fault line opening up inside of me. On one side was the person I was pretending to be in order to function in society. On the other side was the person I actually was, and this person was dying.

The laptop finally stopped buffering. I sat on the edge of the bed with it on my knees, sipping black coffee and comparing myself to other people on Facebook: people I grew up with who were on skiing holidays with their children; people I went to university with who had houses and husbands and jobs; happy, suntanned, all-American girls who lived on the beach in California with men I used to love. I muttered a little prayer. Dear Universe . . .

I went on Google Earth and zoomed out until I found the cliffs that were in my dream, then I zoomed in to the specific corners of the peninsula that still felt like home, even though I hadn't lived there for a while. It was midsummer on Google Earth. The sea was calm and the hedges were full of flowers. I found the car park above the beach where I used to sleep in the Iveco, before someone fell over on the steps and sued the owners and they had to tighten up the rules to cover the cost of public-liability insurance. I found the lay-by above the cove, another spot where I used to sleep in the Iveco, until the owner – a lord who lived in a castle on an island – put up signs in all the lay-bys, directing people to the car park, where he had installed a pay-and-display machine. The lord owned more than just a car park and a castle. He owned thousands of acres of farmland, cliffs and beaches, boulders, hedges, fields, lanes and cottages.

I travelled through time as well as space. I went to my old primary school. It only had thirty pupils when I was there, but now it had even fewer, and a part-time head, and it was periodically threatened with closure. I went to my secondary school, which had fallen into special measures, partly because teachers kept leaving. You couldn't afford a house on a teacher's salary. I found the static caravan where I left my ex-boyfriend. I found the backpackers' hostel where we all used to live in tents and sheds, before it was sold and the sheds were knocked down to make way for an outdoor dining area.

I found the crossroads where Dad's old office was slowly rotting back into the ground. Calling it an office made the warped corrugated-iron structure sound much grander than it actually was. It had been falling down for the best part of two decades. Even before it started falling down, it was just a kind of shed, with walls of wooden tongue and groove, and a shell of rusting metal, and a cavity in between, where the insulation ought to be.

Nearly a decade ago, when I was suddenly homeless, I slept on the floor of the office in a sleeping bag. It was dusty and had no electricity, and Dad's things were still there, untouched and covered in cobwebs, as if he'd gone out for milk and got caught in a tsunami and had never come back. But there was an outside tap nailed to the wooden fence that divided the building from the two allotments that backed on to it, and it was quiet, and it was free – until someone reported me, and a lady from the council came and said I wasn't allowed to sleep there, which is why I moved into a tent.

While I was living in the tent, I saved up for the yellow Iveco, which a friend helped me convert into a camper. The first night I slept alone in the Iveco, I parked it on the crossroads outside the office. This was partly because of the tap, and partly because I was nervous and the office was a place I felt safe. I was woken by policemen in the middle of the night and told I wasn't allowed to park there, because it was too close to a junction. Shortly after that, I left the country for a year, busking from Norway to Portugal. When I returned, I lived in the caravan with my boyfriend, until I left him and moved to Bristol.

I hunched over the laptop. Dad's old office was in a state of advanced decay. The patch of grass in front of the door (I remembered helping to lay the turf) had grown tall and tangled and gone to seed. There was rubbish and junk where Dad used to park his car. I zoomed in. One of the windows was cracked, a piece of guttering had come loose and hung in front of the door, the corrugated iron was rusty and bits of it were caught in the breeze. It was an eyesore. I was surprised the people who lived on the crossroads in their tidy granite or pebble-dash houses hadn't tried to get it torn down. Or perhaps they had. Dad wasn't very good at answering letters, or opening them.

I picked up my guitar and started singing:

> *I'm homesick for the great unfinished emptiness*
> *All those imaginary adventures that I can't forget.*

I heard the front door open and close, voices in the kitchen. I stopped singing, put the guitar back in the corner where it lived, picked up my keys and walked to the river, past the block of still-unlet apartments designed to look like a cruise ship. In real life it was February. The world was cold and grey. I sat on an old flight of steps next to a red brick warehouse that was built to store the cotton and rum from the colonies, brought up the gorge on ships that were also used to carry slaves from Africa to the Americas. These days, the warehouse stored the excess stuff people couldn't fit in their houses, or the stuff belonging to people who didn't have houses. The steps were my favourite place. I had even considered renting a storage unit and living in it. Storage units were much cheaper than the box room, and I would have it all to myself. But the owners of storage units were already wise to the possibility of people trying to live in them. The warehouse was covered in signs and padlocks and CCTV.

It was low tide. The river was full of upturned shopping trolleys. Their wheels were spinning in the breeze, like the windmills of a tiny offshore wind farm. I pulled my phone out of my pocket and tried to call Dad. I wanted to know who owned his old office and why they were leaving it to rot. An automated voice told me Dad's number was no longer available.

I stared at the river drifting lazily past me towards the sea, the landlocked herring gulls balancing on the great mountains of mud, mudlarking, making the most of it, finding everything they needed for their survival. They didn't seem to care that the sea was miles away. I stood up and walked down to the water's edge, as close as I could get, close enough to smell the mud. The gulls panicked and flew away, flapping and shrieking. The wheels on the shopping trolleys kept on spinning.

I left the river and walked slowly back to the house. I didn't stare at the empty apartments in the new block that was designed to look like a cruise ship. I didn't stick two fingers up at the signs in front of them saying *No dogs* and *No ball games*.

I didn't notice the car when I crossed the road by Asda until it nearly ran me over. I didn't pay attention to the man in the street, shaking his head. I didn't feel sad about the tents in the trees or enraged by the billboards showing glossy young couples drinking wine in luxury apartments that hadn't been built yet.

I let myself in and shut the door behind me and went and sat on the edge of my bed. I stood up and went to my window and twisted my neck until I could see a tiny slice of sky. I couldn't win this game. The odds were stacked against me. The only thing I could do was refuse to play.

But how?

In my mind's eye I saw the crossroads, where Dad's old office had been forgotten and abandoned, like the wrecked hull of a boat. I saw myself opening the door, stepping inside, closing the door, listening to the silence. I saw myself waking up, going outside, listening to the birds.

I remembered how Dad used to say that possession is nine points of the law. I still didn't know exactly what it meant.

But I did know exactly where the key to his old office was hidden.

Clothing

A man who has at last found something to do will
not need to get a new suit to do it in.

I was the last person to move into the house I shared with four other adults and a child. Everyone who moved in before me took the furniture they didn't like out of their rooms and put it in the box room. When the box room became my room, I took out the furniture I didn't like and put it in the lean-to, which shared a wall with the box room. The lean-to was also home to the washing machine, which was a bone of contention because the washing machine was very noisy and my housemates were forever putting it on before they went to bed, meaning that I would be woken in the small hours by the sound of the spin cycle. Where I was going, there would be no washing machine. I made sure to do all my laundry before I left.

I owned many more items of clothing than I actually wore. They languished in a massive wooden wardrobe that was too big to fit in the lean-to. I had tipped the wardrobe over, because I couldn't stand it looming darkly in the corner and casting a shadow over everything. It was marginally less oppressive on its side, where it also functioned as a surface for the random pieces of junk that stuck to me like burrs until I picked them off and left them on the wardrobe to gather dust. Foreign coins and old Oyster cards and batteries that might or might not be dead, and CDs that wouldn't play, and foreign adaptor plugs and takeaway menus and phone numbers and pieces of surf wax that were so small they were useless.

Once I had decided what to do, it all happened very fast. My plan was not sensible or wise or legal or financially sound. It was a castle in the air, made of images from Google Earth and half-forgotten memories from childhood, and a yearning so strong it had no name. The forces within me, which had been gathering and building like the steam in a pressure cooker, finally overwhelmed the forces bearing down on me. I found someone to sublet my room, told my various clients I was leaving, and tried and failed to get hold of Dad. The rising tide of desperation drowned out the voices of anxiety. I told myself that, if my half-formed plan didn't work, I could come back to the box room. Or go back to living in a tent. Or save and save and buy another van like my beloved Iveco, which had been crushed into a cube and shipped to China because its bodywork fell apart.

My housemates were surprised by my decision. For them, it was only in the city that life had purpose and significance. Nothing happened in the country. You needed to be in the bustling centre of things, where people collected together to buy and sell and strive and dance and bounce ideas off each other. I'd find my way in the end, they said. These things took time. I understood the pull of the city, how it could make life feel bigger, but I couldn't shake the feeling that life was getting smaller and time was running out. The things I wanted were impossible in the box room. I could not wake up every morning to the sound of people shouting at each other in the kitchen and spend all my energy worrying about how I was going to pay the rent.

I began by transferring the contents of the wardrobe into five bin bags and loading them into the tatty silver Peugeot 306 that my ex-boyfriend had given me before we split up. It was a daunting task. The contents of the wardrobe were a tangled mess of high-heeled shoes and odd socks and muddy items of fancy dress last seen late at night in a field, when I was high and wrecked and happy. There were wigs and tights and fishnet stockings. There were flared jeans and ironic jumpers saying *LOL,* and broken plastic hangers. There were clothes with sentimental value, and clothes with no value whatsoever – out-of-shape acrylic jumpers made in Bangladesh for Primark and then given to a charity shop and then bought by me and worn for a week before being stuffed into the wardrobe and forgotten.

Having all these superfluous clothes was not just a problem for me, it was a problem for the planet. Every time I washed my out-of-shape acrylic jumpers and my old fleeces, the plastic microfibres they were made of were released into the ocean, via the washing machine. They even found their way into the food I ate.[9]

At least I wasn't going to be accidentally eating the two ancient sheepskin coats that had been handed down to me by my dead grandmothers. It struck me that these coats, which had outlived both my grandmothers, would probably outlive me too. And not as plastic microfibres either, but as actual coats.

By the time I had finished taking everything out of my room and putting it in my car, it was so overloaded I couldn't see anything at all out of the back windscreen. I said a final goodbye to my housemates and we all promised to keep in touch, even though we all knew we probably wouldn't. The silver Peugeot had a kind of involuntary tic that caused the indicators to come on willy-nilly and refuse to turn off again. This was dangerous and stressful on a motorway, but since I didn't have the money to pay a mechanic to fix them, all I could do was kiss the steering wheel and pray.

The girl I had found to sublet the box room was younger than I was. She had seemed excited at the prospect of sharing with four other adults and a child.

'Where are you going?' she asked me.

'I'm going to squat in a shed that used to be my dad's office,' I said.

I bit my lip. Please let the key be in the same place it always was. Please let the water not have been turned off.

'Just for a bit. I'm going to write a book.'

Fake it till you make it.

'That sounds cool,' said the girl, who had dark curly hair and freckles. 'Where is it?'

'It's on the far side of Land's End,' I said.

'Oh,' she said. 'Wow.'

The far side of Land's End is a long way from anywhere. It was dusk by the time I finally parked the silver Peugeot next to the black and white chevron signs that had been placed in front of the shed by the council to warn drivers about the ninety-degree bend in the road. The sky was light around the edges, as it often is at dusk in early spring, as though the sun is limbering up, getting ready to breathe life back into the comatose world.

I kissed the steering wheel again, out of gratitude, even though the right-hand indicator was still flashing, which meant the battery would probably be dead in the morning. I climbed out of the car, stretched my legs, smelled the salt in the air and took a deep breath. This was the moment of truth, the moment when my plans would become reality – or not. I felt a rush of adrenaline. It was hard to breathe. I felt like I'd swallowed a stone and now someone was squeezing me around the waist. If the key wasn't in its place under the granite boulder, then I would try to break in, and if I couldn't break in, I would call my big sister and ask if I could sleep on her sofa until I got myself sorted out. I took another deep breath, clasped my shaking hands together and said, 'Right.'

The key was under the boulder, but it was so rusty it wouldn't fit in the lock. As it happened, this didn't matter, because, when I tried to force it, the lock came off in my hands. The door was so rotten it could no longer hold the screws. I pushed the rotten door inwards. Spider webs crackled and stuck to my face.

There was the sound of panic-stricken creatures scrabbling to get back into the wall cavities. I stepped into the darkness and waited for my eyes to adjust. The smell was overpowering: a heady mixture of damp wood and rust and woodworm dust and ammonia, which Dad had used for printing his plans. I could smell the instant coffee Dad used to drink with a brand of powdered milk called Marvel. I wasn't sure if the smell was in the building or in my head. How could it still smell of Dad's instant coffee after all this time?

When my eyes adjusted to the gloomy darkness, I saw that the old shed looked the same, too. The same as it had when I slept in it, briefly, a decade ago. The same as it had when I was ten years old. Nobody had been there. The files from Dad's business were still stacked in cardboard boxes on the floor. When I went closer, I saw that the boxes and the files stored in them had been partly shredded and eaten by mice. Dad's things were still on the wide wooden shelves: set squares and protractors and rulers, and pencil leads in hexagonal plastic boxes, objects that were painfully familiar, yet also looked as if they belonged in a museum. How could so much time have passed? How could the world have changed so radically in my short lifetime? Nobody we knew owned a computer when Dad had his business. If the internet had been invented, then hardly anybody had ever heard of it. When I went with Dad to measure up for his plans, we used a wooden tripod and a surveying microscope that was kept in a wooden box lined with green velvet, with a receipt dated March 1948.

Dad's drawing board was still there. There was a plan taped to it, although it was covered in a layer of dust so thick it was impossible to see the outline of the house Dad had been inventing. There was the little table in the corner, where I used to sit and colour in the trees on the plans and count paperclips and worry about the meaning of the word 'pending', which was the name of one of the trays in the stack on the desk: *In*, *Out* and *Pending*.

I was very tired. I went outside and fought my way through the overgrown patch of ground to the south of the shed. The shed occupied a tiny triangle of land; the hypotenuse was a granite wall, out of which cascaded all sorts of vegetation. There was gorse, bindweed, ferns, brambles, two different kinds of roses and even a twisted crab-apple tree. The short edge of the triangle was the end of the shed itself, which led west to a rotting wooden fence that separated the shed and the tiny plot of land it stood on from two allotments that belonged to two fishermen. The shed belonged to these fishermen, who were cousins, before it belonged to Dad. It was built for their Aunty Gladys, who had it as a sweet shop, back when there were still enough children in the village to make selling sweets worthwhile. If I stood in the middle of the road, behind where I parked the car, I could still just about make out the word S H O P painted on to the corrugated roof. Between being a sweet shop and being abandoned, the shed had been a grocer's, a beach shop, an art gallery, a shoemaker's, a weaver's, a baker's, a clockmaker's, and Dad's.

I fought my way through head-high nettles and thistles and brambles to the rotting fence. I found the tap and turned it on. Water came out. Reeling with relief, I went to the car and saw that the indicator had stopped flashing. I found my hot-water bottle and camping stove and the little camping kettle I'd bought in a town called Enontekiö, in Finnish Lapland. I had forgotten to buy candles. When it got too dark, I used the light from my mobile phone. I made myself a bed in the middle of the floor, out of my surfboard bag and my sleeping bag. I made a hot-water bottle and put it in the sleeping bag. I went outside to clean my teeth. There was a handful of stars in the dark blue sky. I pretended I had only seen one of them so I could close my eyes and make a wish.

> Star light, star bright,
> First star I see tonight,
> I wish I may, I wish I might,
> Have this wish I wish tonight.

It was very quiet outside, and very quiet inside, apart from the occasional sound of a car approaching and slowing for the bend and then accelerating away, and the sound of footsteps coming and going along the road, and pausing to inspect my car and wonder what it was doing there, and the sound of the geese that lived on the pond responding to the owner of the footsteps. The uninsulated walls were very thin, so all of these sounds were very loud. I lay in the darkness and, the longer I lay there listening, the more sounds I heard. I heard the creatures that lived in the wall cavities running up and down on their little feet. Even though I knew they were mice, and I knew you weren't supposed to like mice, I found the noise of these tiny creatures comforting. Mum introduced me to camping before I could walk, and I had spent much of my adult life living in tents and vans. There was something familiar about being on the floor in a sleeping bag. I fell into a deep and dreamless sleep.

When I woke there was light seeping through the gap under the door and pooling on the floor. It was very quiet. I pulled myself into a sitting position on the surfboard bag, which had turned out to be a surprisingly comfortable bed. I wriggled out of the sleeping bag and stood up and walked over to the big window next to the door, pulling the cord to open the brown metal blind. The blind didn't open. Instead, it came off the wall altogether. Behind it were the well-established habitats of half a dozen huge black spiders. My fear of spiders is embedded in my ancient reptilian brain, which doesn't respond to logic. My screams must have been audible on the other side of the village. I clamped a hand over my mouth, remembering I didn't want anyone to know I was there. The spiders shrank back into their hammocky nests. I hauled the door open and ran outside into the road. I could tell from the colour of the sky that it was still much too early to call my sister.

I plugged my phone into the charger in the car and went to use the toilets on the cricket field, which was a hundred yards from my shed, back up the road I had driven down the previous evening. I knew these toilets well; I had used them the previous time I slept in the shed, and when I lived in the Iveco. I went through the gate into the cricket field and pushed the door to the toilets, but it didn't open. I tried again. It still didn't open. The toilets on the cricket field were locked.

I tried to remember where the next nearest public toilets were located. I thought there were some in the cove at the end of the lane that led south from the crossroads. I walked back to the shed and set off down the lane towards the cove. I knew that a three-mile round trip just to use the toilet was not sustainable, but neither was squatting in Dad's old office. It was a temporary solution, a stopgap, a shed. There was no electricity, no toilet, no heating and no shower. The door didn't lock. It was full of mice and spiders and the chewed remains of Dad's business. It smelled of loss. I didn't even know who owned it.

The overgrown hedges on both sides of the lane that led down to the cove were singing. Sparrows and wrens and swallows darted in and out of the gorse and the blackthorn and the hawthorn. There was a blackbird on the telegraph wires, singing its heart out. I stopped to pick a yellow gorse flower, rubbing it between my fingers to smell the coconut. The blackthorn had already started flowering in places, the dead-looking twigs surging unexpectedly into life. When I squinted at it, the blackthorn seemed to be frothing. The road was covered in white petals, like a dusting of snow, or confetti left over from a wedding. Daffodils marched in rows through the fields. From my days as a flower picker, I knew they had flowered too early

– they had 'blown' and would be left to rot. In other fields, single daffodils, whose bulbs had somehow survived the huge machines that were sent in to plough them up, waved frantically from the rows of cabbages and cauliflowers, like drowning swimmers. And then, suddenly, there was the sea, the endless glinting ocean, stretching in front of me forever, mingling its colours with the sky so I couldn't tell where one ended and the other started. I leaned over a rusty gate to watch the sun rise out of the water like a giant red balloon.

I reached the lay-by where I used to park the Iveco, side door facing east, so I could watch the sun rise without getting out of bed. I found the sign I'd seen on Google Earth: *Passing Place, No Parking Please*. In the bottom right-hand corner was the estate logo, as if the man who lived in the castle on the island wasn't a human being, who might be expected to bear some responsibility for the place and the community, but an anonymous corporation that could not be expected to care about anything except money.

There were more signs in the cove, arrows protruding from a wooden post, pointing to the car park and the cliffs, the tiny beach covered in seaweed, the cafe. The signs turned the old familiar cove into a kind of theme park. They seemed to suggest that the ancient cliffs had been placed there by the benevolent lord and his estate for the benefit of tourists, rather than evolving over millennia, created by forces far beyond the capacity of humans: volcanoes, plate tectonics, the shattering of continents, storms, swells, ice ages. The signs all had the estate logo on them. I walked up to the pay-and-display machine in the car park. It was four pounds to park for a whole day and two pounds to park for two hours.

In the seventeenth century, there was a group of activists, called the Diggers, who fought for the right to farm on common land.

The Work we are going about is this, To dig up Georges-Hill and the waste Ground thereabouts, and to Sow Corn, and to eat our bread together by the sweat of our brows. And the First Reason is this, That we may work in righteousness, and lay the Foundation of making the Earth a Common Treasury for All, both Rich and Poor, That every one that is born in the land, may be fed by the Earth his Mother that brought him forth, according to the Reason that rules in the Creation. Not Inclosing any part into any particular hand, but all as one man, working together, and feeding together as Sons of one Father, members of one Family; not one Lording over another, but all looking upon each other, as equals in the Creation.[10]

In 2012, a modern group calling themselves Diggers 2012 set up camp on a piece of abandoned ground at the Runnymede Campus of Brunel University. Runnymede was the place where King John signed the Magna Carta, which put commoners' rights into law, although most of these rights have since been eroded. The land the modern Diggers occupied had been unused for six years. The Diggers called it Runnymede Eco Village. They were forcibly evicted, because the unused land was earmarked by developers for luxury flats.[11]

One way to make the earth a common treasury for all, both rich and poor, would be to introduce a land tax.[12] The revenue could be invested in a sovereign wealth fund that could one day fund a Universal Basic Income[13] – the modern equivalent of the right to farm the commons, ensuring that 'every one that is born in the land may be fed by the Earth his Mother that brought him forth'. In his book, *All That is Solid: The Great Housing Disaster*, Danny Dorling explains how not having a land tax is one of the factors underpinning serious economic inequality: 'when land prices rise, as they have risen in the UK, someone is making a mint out of doing nothing but starting off rich. Only those who start off rich can own great quantities of land and then buy more.'[14]

The lord's fields and car parks and cottages had an intrinsic value that was not related to anything he had done. It was linked to natural resources like the sea, which meant people wanted to come and visit the cove, and public investment in things like roads, which meant they could. It was linked to public investment in clean beaches and public toilets, which, mercifully, weren't locked. The lack of a land tax in the UK means that the vast majority of people have no stake in the land, receive no benefit from it, and usually have to pay through the nose to access it. The earth, our common treasury, is divided extremely unequally between wealthy landowners and everybody else.

On the way back to the shed, I thought about calling my sister. I planned what I would say and tried to work out how she would react to the news that I had spent the night in Dad's old office. My big sister and I are close in age and close as people, almost like twins, but somewhere along the way our paths had diverged. Sometimes it seemed to me that we were side by side, stuck together, but navigating completely different realities. What was incomprehensible to me was often obvious to her, and vice versa.

My sister was not afraid of spiders, for example. As far as I could tell, she was not afraid of anything, although she insisted she was terrified of moths and thunderstorms and fireworks, and that sometimes she lay awake at night convinced the sky was about to fall in. I didn't believe it for a minute. She was a lifeguard and a coastguard and the first person I called when I was in trouble.

There was no reception inside the shed. I went outside and stood on the concrete doorstep, leaning back against the corrugated iron.

My sister answered after two rings.

'What on earth are you doing in Dad's old office?' she said, before I could even speak.

Someone had seen my car and she had put two and two together. I had forgotten she knew everything. Big sisters always do. It was why I tried to come over braver and stronger than I actually felt when I was around our little sister. I worried that our little sister thought *I* knew everything, too.

My big sister didn't just know every*thing*, she knew every*one*. Both my sisters knew everyone, and people who knew the two of them were often amazed to find out I existed. I wasn't sure why I had always tried to be invisible. My place in the community was a riddle I had never solved, a source of anxiety and paranoia. I didn't fit in here, but I didn't fit in anywhere else, either. The landscape was home, but I was convinced the people who occupied it didn't approve of me. I thought of them like gods, sitting in judgement, waiting to send me into everlasting exile. At least in the city I could be anonymous. Here, I stuck out like a sore thumb. Even my clothes were all wrong.

'I would have called you,' I said, 'but I thought you might try to talk me out of it.'

'Talk you out of what?'

'Living in the office.'

'You're going to *live* there?'

'No, I mean, I'm just going to sleep in it for a bit, until I find somewhere to live.'

'You're moving back down?'

'Yes.'

'That's amazing.'

'I thought it might be embarrassing for the kids.'

'What, you moving back down?'

'No, sleeping in the office. You remember the people who lived in those old buses on the field behind the community centre when we were at primary school? We used to think they were seriously weird.'

'They were.'

'Maybe they weren't. Maybe they just didn't want to pay rent.'

I let myself slide down the corrugated iron until I was sitting on the concrete step.

'Have you spoken to Dad?'

'Not yet. The number I've got for him doesn't work.'

'Did you break in?'

'The key was in the same place. Not that I needed it. The door is so rotten, the lock fell out. Nobody's been here for decades.'

'Someone's bound to tell the council. They probably already have.'

'I know. I won't get away with it for long. Plus there's loads of massive spiders.'

'Do you want me to come over?'

'Can you?'

'After I've dropped the kids off at school.'

'I love you.'

I rummaged through the bags of stuff in the car until I found my espresso maker. I made coffee on the tiny gas stove, staring at the spiders the whole time, in case they moved. I drank it sitting on the concrete doorstep, watching sparrows and wrens bustling in and out of the overflowing hedge, and swallows diving in the sky.

My sister parked her van behind my car.

'Nice packing,' she said, pointing to the black plastic bin bags that were pressed up against the back windscreen.

'I didn't have much time to sort stuff out,' I said.

'Why?' she said, hugging me. 'Did you get into trouble with loan sharks, or sleep with someone's boyfriend, or rob a bank?'

'No. Course not. I just knew that, if I started to think about it, I probably wouldn't leave. I don't exactly know what I'm going to do.'

I waited outside, a safe distance from the door, while my sister scooped up the spiders whose nests I'd exposed and carried them one by one into the field on the other side of the road. Then she removed the blinds from the other two windows and dealt with their spiders, too.

'Shall I take the blinds and put them in my wheelie bin?' she said, when she had finished.

'Yes, please.'

'You'll have to pin something up over the windows facing the road.'

I'd already thought of that. 'I'll use the clothes I never wear.'

We went inside. There was a loud scuffling coming from the corner of the room where the cardboard boxes were stacked.

'Ssh,' said my sister, holding up her finger.

The animal came out slowly. It knew we were there, but not what we meant. It stopped to rest on its haunches and lick its paws. It was brown and furry and as big as a kitten. It looked like the sort of animal that was used to getting its own way.

'Mouse,' I whispered.

My sister snorted. The animal darted back into the shadows. 'That's not a mouse,' she said. 'That's a rat.'

I spent the rest of the morning sweeping, using an old broom I found in the corner next to Dad's wooden tripod. The broom had lost most of its bristles and I made slow progress, but it took my mind off the fact that I didn't know what I was going to do and there was no easy way back to what I had been doing, at least not for three months, which was how long I had sublet my room. I collected piles and piles of dust and mouse and rat droppings and swept them out of the front door. When I had finished sweeping, I removed the plan and rolled it up and took the drawing board apart and leaned it against the north-facing end of the shed. I unloaded the car, piling up my things in the space where the drawing board had been. There was my cello in its heavy plywood case, and my two guitars, and the daffodil crates full of books. There was all the stuff that would be useless without electricity: records and turntables and mixer and CD drive and laptop and speakers. There were boxes of notebooks and boxes of clutter and boxes of things that would be pointless without a bathroom, like razors and tweezers and shower caps. I owned a lot of things and almost all of them were useless. I carried the bin bags full of clothes in and added them to the pile. Then I carried them back to the car. I would never wear these clothes again. The kindest thing would be to take them to Penzance and donate them to a charity shop.

I drove to the Costcutter, which was three miles away, in my sister's village, and bought cloths and lemon-scented cleaning fluid. I spent an hour wiping the mould and dust off the walls and the shelves. On the shelf with the set squares and pencil leads, I found two photographs in gilt frames. One was of Mum and Dad on their own, and one was of the five of us. Me and my big sister were about six and seven, my little sister was about two. I remembered having the pictures taken. We had gone to a photographer's studio, and Mum had worn make-up.

The photographs belonged to a different reality. Looking at them was painful, like remembering the good parts of a relationship after it had ended. I felt very sad for my parents. They had been so full of ideals, so innocent and vulnerable. They had risked a lot, bringing us to the peninsula, and they had lost everything. I wiped the dust off the photographs and put them face down on the shelf. I had spent years trying not to think about all of this, but, being there in Dad's old office, with the smells and the familiar objects, it was impossible not to remember. I tried to let the thoughts come and go without getting emotionally involved in them.

When I had finished wiping, I pinned up some of my own photographs. The one of my cello by the fjord in the Arctic Circle, and the Ansel Adams one of a black and white river winding its way between black and white mountains into the black and white distance. I found the green and gold ribbons that Hanna, the girl I met at Knivskellodden, told me represented fearlessness. I pinned them to the tongue and groove near the front door, where they fluttered in the wind that blew into the shed through all the cracks in the walls.

I began to go through the contents of Dad's cardboard boxes. There were files relating to various extensions and renovations that Dad had designed and built. I remembered some of the names of some of the houses and the clients. Some of them still lived in the village, as far as I knew; they still drank in the pub. There were letters to the bank and letters to the Inland Revenue. There was a box of diaries, one for all the years until 1992, when the diaries abruptly stopped. I realized that I had been wrong about Dad not opening letters. He had opened and replied to hundreds when he was trying to save his business. He had replied to dozens of letters from the official receiver when his business finally became unsaveable, and then one day he had given up. In the very last box, there was a blue folder full of papers, marked with Dad's distinctive handwriting: *Bankruptcy*.

Shelter

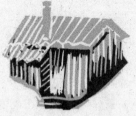

An average house in the neighbourhood costs perhaps
eight hundred dollars, and to lay up this sum will take
from ten to fifteen years of the labourer's life, even if
he is not encumbered with a family.

It was raining light; luminous sheets were moving towards me across the sea, carried by water that had fallen out of dark clouds that were gathering on the horizon.

I was sitting in the mouth of a cave. The cave was at the back of a beach that was at the end of the lane that led west from the crossroads. Unlike the lane that led south, this lane went absolutely straight for half a mile. There was a line of maritime and Monterey pines on the north side of it. The pines were tall and had thick, gnarled trunks. They smelled of sap, like trees in hot, foreign places do, and they provided shelter from cold northerly winds. The pines were the only tall trees within walking distance of the shed. Everything else that tried to grow upwards was stunted and bent by the constant pressure of the wind.

I'd let the track take me down its convoluted path towards the sea. The air tasted of salt. There were four big houses between the farmhouse and the west-facing beach. Only one of them was lived in. The largest one, which was rumoured to have an indoor swimming pool, was somebody's second home. The other two belonged to the lord. They had signs in the windows with the estate logo and website, advertising the fact that they were available for holidays.

After the last house, the track became a footpath, then a flight of wooden steps that dropped down to a great pile of granite boulders. Every few years, a big storm dumped a load of sand on top of the boulders and, for a brief period, the beach turned family friendly. Visitors who had never been there before thought they'd stumbled on a secret and took to hiking down with disposable barbecues, and games of bat and ball. Then the sand would suddenly disappear overnight and the beach would revert, like a hag, to its normal hostile state of slippery rocks and seaweed, unpredictable currents, heavy waves, flotsam, jetsam and flies.

I liked the beach in its hostile state. The seals liked it, too. You could see them basking and fishing in the coves and bays that were sheltered by sheer cliffs. When I swam from this beach, pushing off the rocks, I was almost always greeted by a curious seal. When it was too rough to push off the rocks, which was often, I lay down in a natural pool in front of an arch in the cliffs, cut by the sea. But I was trying not to think about swimming. There was a cold north wind and I didn't have a towel. My sisters both insisted that towels were for pussies, but I hadn't been back for long enough to adjust to their way of thinking.

The cave was invisible from the coast path, because it was

underneath the overhanging cliff. When I was a child, I used to imagine running away and living in this cave, wrapping myself up in seaweed at night, like the seal pups in my favourite book. It's a good thing I didn't, because the cave fills up with water at high tide and it's most likely I would have drowned. Since I last visited the cave, several years ago, boulders had gathered in its mouth, like teeth. There was a small patch of wet sand in front of the boulders, where I sat, sheltering from the worst of the wind watching the band of rain travel towards me, heralded these great waterfalls of light that were pouring out of the grey sky and gathering in lakes of silver on the surface of the ocean.

If I had been there between two and three hundred million years ago, I would not have been shivering in the mouth of a cave. I would have been standing in the centre of a mountain range the size of the Himalayas. Like the Himalayas (which are still getting bigger) the mountains that used to tower into the sky on this peninsula were caused by a kind of tectonic traffic accident, when the continents now known as Europe and America slowly crashed into each other, squeezing the land upwards. Then the continents of Europe and America, or rather the plates underneath them, slowly bounced back, away from each other, creating a gap, which we call the Atlantic. The plates are still moving. The Atlantic is widening at a rate of two millimetres per year.

Even the things that seemed the most solid and timeless, like towering cliffs of granite, were in fact in a state of constant flux. It was comforting and also frightening. Frightening because there was nothing to hold on to. Comforting because there was nothing to lose.

The air was thick with the sound of gulls and gannets and guillemots and crows. Behind me, a waterfall was noisily tipping rainwater on to the rocks. Once upon a time, the stream that fed the waterfall was used to turn a mill wheel. Part of the old stone structure that held the wheel was still just about visible, a ghostly reminder of a time when this wild and remote landscape was heavily industrialized, mined and mined and mined for its copper and tin.

The rocky beach was full of memories. Some of the memories were so vivid they felt more like hallucinations. I could see all my different former selves sitting in that exact same spot at the mouth of the cave, sheltering from emotional storms, as well as meteorological ones. I wondered what happened to these sorts of memories when a place was destroyed by war, or rising sea levels, or development. The farmer who owned this beach, before he died and it passed to his daughter, once tried to get planning permission to build a car park, toilets and a cafe. I used to think that, if permission was granted, I would lie down in front of the diggers and die. I used to write songs about this beach.

> *I know a place that will hold me safe,*
> *under the darkening sky*
> *Where the birds fly up and over, high,*
> *and the old caves watch with their old cave eyes.*

I rested my chin on my knees and watched a container ship motor into a pool of light and then out of it again. For a few moments, the ship was part of an epic piece of theatre, with the sun as a spotlight, manned by some great celestial lighting director. Or perhaps the sun was a searchlight; someone had been looking for that particular ship and now they had found it. Something inside me wanted to be on that ship, travelling. Not that container ships are especially romantic places. The kind of diesel that container ships burn in their engines is banned on land, because the exhaust is so toxic.

I was thinking about Dad. Among the papers in the office, I had found a folder full of plans and planning applications to convert the office into a dwelling. I had looked up the word 'dwelling' in my massive dictionary, peering at it through the magnifying glass.

The word 'dwell' comes from the Old English *dwellan*, which means to mislead or deceive, the Old German *dwelan*, which means to go or lead astray, the Old Norse *dvol*, which means to delay, or *dvali*, which means sleep, the Middle Dutch *dwellen*, which means stun or perplex, and the Old Danish *dvale*, which means trance or stupor. Ultimately, it comes from the Indo-European root *dheu*, which means dust, cloud, vapour or smoke. It wasn't until the middle of the thirteenth century that the word 'dwell' started to mean a place to live in, a home. I couldn't work out how a word that started off meaning dust, cloud, vapour or smoke could end up meaning *home*.

The planning applications had all been refused. If they hadn't been refused, then perhaps Dad wouldn't have gone bankrupt. If Dad hadn't gone bankrupt, then perhaps I wouldn't have been sitting in the mouth of that cave on a cold windy day at the end of March, thinking about the word 'dwell' and how my home *was* a strangely vaporous place, full of mist and water and shifting patterns of light.

I walked down to the edge of the sea, which was a heaving mass of energy. It reminded me of an animal breathing. The water slapped up against the rocks, then retreated – in, out, in, out – like the pulsing of a massive heart. Anyone who has spent any length of time in close proximity to the ocean will understand its magnetism. It beckons you in, seducing you, tempting you to get naked, making you yearn for the velvet touch of water on your skin. Before long, I succumbed. I knew I would. It was partly the fact that I hadn't had a shower for two weeks, only brief and freezing washes under the outside tap. I felt dirty. I wanted to wash off the thoughts and the memories and the letters and the file marked *Bankruptcy* and the burned bridges and the gnawing sense of failure that came with being back in this place again, the place I had tried so hard to escape.

When I was a teenager, I was convinced that life was happening somewhere else. I was keen to find this other place and reinvent myself in it. I wanted to go where nobody knew me. I wanted to leave behind all the things I didn't like about myself and my history. As soon as I was old enough, I moved abroad. I lived in Italy. I lived in France. I travelled to South America. But, no matter how far I went and how long I stayed there, it always felt temporary. I couldn't settle. I would feel a thirst for the specific landscape of this peninsula, and the thirst would grow and grow until it dragged me back to living in a tent or a van where there was no work and no money and the air smelled of failure.

I peeled off my thick Norwegian jumper, then I pulled off my shoes, socks, tracksuit trousers and T-shirt and shivered through the cold air until I reached the pool in front of the arch. The pool had a depth of about six feet, but the water was so clear I could see the seaweed and the pebbles at the bottom, and the various slimy creatures that lived among the rocks, floating in and out with the tide, living lives of total surrender. I slid under the water, gasping and flailing my arms around with the shock of it. I floated on my back for thirty seconds, staring up at the grey clouds, then I got out and clambered back over the boulders to my clothes.

I felt warm, standing naked on the rocks in the cold north wind. My skin tingled with life. I put my clothes on without drying myself, which didn't matter at all because the great wall of rain that had been travelling towards me for the past hour hit while I was walking back up the steps, and by the time I got back to the shed I was soaked to the skin.

The shed was dark and gloomy. In the afternoons and evenings, all the light gathered in the west, and there was no window in the west-facing wall. I lit three candles, then took off my wet clothes and spread them on the floorboards to dry. I put my pyjamas on and made a hot-water bottle and a cup of tea and got into my sleeping bag. The rain sounded like gunfire on the old tin roof. It was the first serious rain since I had begun sleeping in the shed and I had yet to find out if the roof was watertight. I held my mug of tea in both of my hands, to warm them up, leaning back against the tongue-and-groove wall. I could feel the boards sucking in and out with the gusts of wind, like the canvas sides of a tent. The candle flames flickered madly in the cross-currents of draughts from the gaps between the boards and the gaps around the window and under the door. In the *Three Little Pigs*, the big bad wolf blows down the houses made of sticks and straw. Only the one made of bricks survives.

I tried to read, but the candles were flickering so much, reading was impossible. I stared into space. I'd deliberately not allowed myself much time for thinking since I left Bristol. I'd been surfing, engaging with the frustration of being horribly out of practice. I'd caught up with friends and family. I'd seen Mum, and heard about her latest housing troubles. She was facing the prospect of another inspection by *her* letting agent. The woman who owned the flat she rented had recently died and the flat had passed to her children, who lived elsewhere. It hurt to see the fright in Mum's eyes.

Soon, the storm got so noisy that even thinking was impossible. With their thick stone walls and double-glazing, houses provide insulation from the sound of the raging world just as much as from the actual effects of rain and heat and cold. The shed had no insulation and the sounds were as loud inside as they were outside. Louder, if anything. All I could do was crouch on the surfboard bag and try to identify the sources of the sudden and violent noises.

The big bad wolf huffed and puffed. The shed rattled and shook and creaked and groaned. The walls strained. The floorboards trembled. The energy of the storm was transferred, via the floorboards, to my own body. I felt myself vibrating. My green and gold ribbons, which were supposed to represent fearlessness, trembled violently. I felt like I was down below on a little wooden boat, rolling on a big swell. Or perhaps it was more like being inside a tin can that was being kicked down a potholed track.

In the early hours of the morning, there was a single, very loud clap of thunder. Shortly afterwards, I went outside. It was cold and I couldn't sleep, and I needed water to make a hot-water bottle. The storm seemed less violent outside than it did inside, where the shed was mounting its rattling, shaking, noisy defence against the elements. Outside, the storm had the run of the place. Unchallenged, it seemed less furious. There was a strange noise floating across the fields, a humming sound, like a male-voice choir. I stood in the overgrown grass behind the chevrons until I worked out that it was only the sound of the electricity cables vibrating in the wind like the strings of a giant guitar.

I filled the kettle with water from the outside tap and fought my way back through the wind to the door. I jammed a piece of cardboard between the door and the frame, to keep it shut. I lit a new candle and balanced the kettle on the tiny camping stove and went over to the corner where I kept my massive dictionary. The word 'storm' is from the Indo-European root *(s)twer*, which means turn or whirl.

When the water in the kettle boiled I made a fresh hot-water bottle and held it against my chest. It was so hot it burned me through my thick jumper. I snuggled into my sleeping bag. The shed had somehow survived the worst of the storm, in spite of all the things that were wrong with it. I started to wonder if maybe I *could* stay there, at least until after the summer. Then I made a mental list of all the reasons I couldn't.

The door didn't close or lock. The floorboards were black with dirt; no amount of sweeping seemed to touch it. The lack of electricity made using a computer problematic, especially one whose battery had expanded and stopped working. It was dark, even in the daytime, because there was no window in the west-facing wall. The west-facing wall needed a door, so I could go in and out to fetch water and wee in the garden, without having to run the gauntlet of the inquisitive residents of the houses on the other side of the crossroads. I needed more shelves and some sort of chest of drawers or clothes rail. I needed a toilet and a shower and a fridge. The window on the south-facing end, the one right above the board bag, needed fixing. The frame was so rotten, it absorbed water like a sponge. When the frame was waterlogged, the excess was pushed out. The upshot was that it was raining on my face. I shuffled the board bag into the corner, away from the leaking window.

I listened to the storm blow itself out, huddling in the

sleeping bag with my hot-water bottle. The shed was still rattling, only much less violently now. I felt a growing sense of wellbeing. I was warm (thanks to the hot-water bottle) and (mostly) dry. My shelter was still standing. For the first time in a long time, in spite of the fact that sleeping in the shed was illegal and I didn't even know who owned it, I felt safe.

Building the House

If you have built castles in the air, your work
need not be lost; that is where they should be.
Now put the foundations under them.

The morning after the storm, the world seemed brand new, as if it had just been invented. I stood in the rain-washed stillness, face tilted towards the sun, listening to a blackbird. The blackbird was singing so loudly, it had woken me up. It was sitting on the telegraph wire that ran along the top of the hedge that was the boundary between my garden and the lane that led down to the cove. I had never taken the time to actually watch a bird singing before. I'd never seen how its whole body expands and contracts to make the sounds, as if the bird is a squeeze box being played by the wind. Singing was a serious business for this blackbird. He took in air with his whole being and then breathed it out as a perfect musical phrase. It looked effortful and totally exhausting. His feathers stood on end with the sheer *work* of every breath. Once, on the radio, I heard someone playing a recording of a blackbird singing. They slowed it right down until it sounded as simple and complicated and religious as Bach.

Inside the shed, my phone was ringing. It was my sister.

'Is the office still standing?'

'Just about.'

'I mentioned to someone at the market that you were looking for somewhere to live and she said she had a flat for rent. It's overlooking the beach.'

I felt a tremor of excitement.

'How much?'

'I don't know. I got her number. I said you'd call her.'

I went to see the flat on Saturday morning. It was a bedsit with beige furniture and a brown carpet and bad art on the walls – the kind of mediocre, inoffensive, utterly bland seaside scenes that are sold in packs of ten prints, ready framed, especially for holiday cottages. It was right next to the beach, but you couldn't see the sea because there was a massive house in front of it. The owner of the flat, who lived in a different county, also owned the massive house. She and her family had used it for holidays, until they bought an even bigger house, a hundred metres away, down the lane. Both of the massive houses were usually empty.

The flat was as dark as the box room had been, because of the massive house right in front of it. There was no outside space, and nothing to see out of the windows apart from the yellow walls of the massive house. But there was a bathroom with a toilet and a shower. It was insulated, and legal, and there didn't seem to be any spiders, or rats. I could imagine living there. It was a relief. In my imagination, I looked like a normal person. There was a Yale lock on the door, and a wheelie bin. The owner told me the rent was £500 a month, plus bills, and I'd have to move out for the Easter holidays, which were four weeks away, and between June and October, because she could make £500 a week renting the flat to tourists.

I thanked her and said I would think about it, then I drove to my sister's house and sat at her kitchen table while she made coffee.

'Well?' she said.

'I think it's impossible,' I said. 'There aren't enough hours in the day to make the rent.'

'Don't be so pathetic. You've got a good degree; you could get a proper job.'

'Such as?'

My sister picked up the *Cornishman* and turned to the jobs section. The jobs section took up less than a page. (Houses had their own forty-page supplement.)

'Cleaning septic tanks,' she said, eventually.

'Cheers.'

'It's really well paid.'

'No thanks.'

'Caring.'

'Sure, but it's minimum wage.'

'True. Still. It would be totally doable if you worked full-time.'

'None of these jobs are full-time.'

'You'd find a way. Other people do. They have to.'

'I know.'

She was right. I could find a way. I could make the necessary sacrifices. I could forget the book I wanted to write and the songs I wanted to record. My sister must have seen the look on my face.

'What about busking?' she said.

'Five hundred a month, plus bills?'

It wasn't even just the money. Even if I did take the flat and found the deposit and made the rent, I'd be back to square one again in a couple of months. I'd have to put all my stuff back in the car and go and live in a tent or something. What was the point?

'I said I'd think about it,' I told my sister, 'and I will.'

I thought about it all the way into Penzance, and I was still thinking about it when I parked my car in the car park behind the greengrocer's that was shortly going to be turned into an estate agent's. Penzance had changed since I was last there. About half the shops on the high street seemed to be estate agents or hairdressers, apart from the ones that were charity shops and the ones that were empty. There was a new Poundland and a new Tesco Metro, but Woolworths had gone and so had Top Shop and Dorothy Perkins. The bargain-basement hardware store called Jim's Cash and Carry was still there. I wandered inside and started collecting things I needed for the shed. I picked out a new broom, with stiff bristles, because the one I had been using had finally fallen apart. I picked up a roll of gaffer tape to try to seal the rat holes. I found a fake-enamel bowl and plate, a plastic knife, fork and spoon, a green plastic mug, a packet of three lighters with pictures of horses on them, five boxes of household candles, five boxes of night lights, a pack of J-cloths, a pack of sponges, a small saucepan, a bottle of washing-up liquid, a plastic washing-up bowl, a bottle of all-purpose cream cleaner, a pair of gardening gloves, a pair of secateurs, a trowel, a garden fork and a big tub of rat poison.

After Jim's Cash and Carry, I went to the bank to ask them to increase my overdraft. I waited a long time in the queue. The man in front of me was wearing yellow sunglasses and clutching a brown satchel. The lady behind the counter spoke loudly to him. I couldn't help overhearing.

'How are you getting on?' she said.

'I'm doing well.' The man swayed slightly. 'Just two or three brandies a night, now. If I have more than three brandies, I'll be in a coma, but you've got to take it one day at a time. Even if you're not going into a coma, you've got to take it one day at a time.'

The bank agreed to increase my overdraft, but said it would cost me a pound a day.

On my way back to the car, I stopped to look in the window of one of the estate agents. There were dozens of pictures of houses. There was nothing special about them. They were just houses. Four walls and a roof. Some of them had gardens. Some of them had garages or parking spaces. What was extraordinary were the numbers underneath the houses. It was as if the prices were written in a different currency.

Curious, I pulled out my phone and googled the average wage for someone working full-time in Cornwall. My phone came back with £17,264. Half the houses in the window were on sale for more than half a million pounds. I ignored the houses in the window and googled the *average* price of a house in Cornwall. My phone came back with £206,323.[15] I typed a little over the average wage – £18,000 – into the Halifax mortgage calculator, and estimated my outgoings at roughly £200 a month. The Halifax mortgage calculator said I would be allowed to borrow £51,000.[16]

Back at the shed, there was a man in the allotment on the other side of the rotting wooden fence with the tap on it. I remembered him as the man who used to drive around the village, selling fish. He kept the fish in buckets of ice in the back of his tiny white van. He'd come to our cottage and Mum would choose the fish she wanted to buy and the man would gut it in front of us, chopping its head off with a special knife and chucking the head in a bucket full of blood and ice, then weighing the fish on a pair of scales. I had been impressed by how the different types of fish seemed to bear no relation to each other; they were as far apart as humans and elephants and kangaroos. The chunky, aerodynamic mackerel with their shimmering stripes; the plaice with their orange spots, so flat they looked like someone had run them over; the crabs with their claws and spidery legs.

I tried to retreat behind the shed before the man saw me, but I was too late. He came over to the fence and leaned on his hoe.

'Staying in there, are you?'

I felt a stab of anxiety, like a little punch in the solar plexus. The fisherman was exactly the kind of person who would sit on the parish council.

'Needs a bit of work.'

'That's true,' I said.

'How's your mother?'

'She's fine.' I lied.

The man straightened up slowly. Even when he was straight, he was bent over. He turned and pointed to a row of turnips at the back of his garden.

'Do you like turnips?'

'Yes,' I said. In fact, it was a long time since I'd eaten a turnip and I couldn't remember if I liked them or not.

He went over to the row of turnips and pulled out three big roots, then came back and passed them to me over the fence. I held the turnips by their leaves, which were rough and scratchy.

'I like them mashed up with butter,' said the man who used to sell fish. And he winked.

I spent the rest of that day dealing with the overgrown garden. I began by attacking it with my new pair of secateurs, gathering brambles and nettles and hogweed into a huge pile in the middle of the small triangle. I tried to dig up a hogweed root using my new trowel, but it was as big as one of the turnips I planned to eat for lunch, and the trowel from Jim's Cash and Carry was made in China and bent backwards like the spoons we used to eat our school dinners with.

I abandoned the hogweed roots and approached the hedge that divided the garden from the lane. It was a Cornish hedge, which means it was a wall made of granite boulders that were held together by earth and plants and time and habit. I was impressed by the sheer variety of plants growing out of the hedge. It seemed amazing to me that all these different forms had found a place to thrive, coexisting, instead of competing each other out of existence. Even the bindweed seemed to know its place – just. There was gorse, blackthorn and honeysuckle. There were roses, foxgloves, ferns, hogweed, dock leaves, goose grass, bluebells and primroses. I pulled out some sticky goose grass and remembered how we used to stick it on each other's bums when we were children, to make tails for ourselves.

A robin came to see what I was up to. He hopped close to me, cocking his head left, right, left, right. Something rustled out of the leaves in the hedge. It was a wren. The wren was about half the size of the robin and twice as loud. Sparrows were flying in and out of the hole at the southern apex of the shed roof, with bits of hedge in their beaks. The sparrows seemed to be building a nest between the metal roof and the tongue-and-groove ceiling. This explained the noises that woke me up every morning, the scratching and tapping that sounded like it was directly above my head. Higher up in the sky, crows and sea-gulls wheeled around and shoved each other off the electricity cables that ran from a wooden pole that jammed up against the north-west corner of the shed to another one at the point of the triangle. Pigeons flapped their wings and gurgled. Somewhere, there was the downward-curving wail of a buzzard.

After I had cut down the worst of the weeds, I gathered up the rubbish that had accumulated in the long grass between the shed and the chevrons. There were crisp packets and beer cans and other things that could have conceivably blown out of the windows of passing cars, and there were things that must have been deliberately dumped there by people who couldn't be bothered to drive to the tip. I found two old car tyres, a pile of broken concrete and a cracked old shower tray. I put the wrappers and the cans and the concrete and the tyres against the north-facing end of the shed, by the lane, ready to load into my car. I dragged the shower tray to the fence and balanced it on rocks underneath the tap, so I could crouch in it when I was washing, instead of having to sit in the nettles and thistles.

I carried the disintegrating cardboard boxes full of mouse-eaten files outside and added them to the pile of weeds. In one of the boxes, I found a set of deeds to the shed. The deeds contained a plan of the property, and a contract signed by Dad and the two fishermen, dated 1985.

I called my sister.

'I found the deeds to the office,' I told her.

'They must be copies,' she said.

'Why?'

'Because the bank took them. Where did you find them, anyway?'

'In the boxes of stuff. I'm having a clear-out. I'm going to have a bonfire.'

'I wouldn't burn anything today. It's much too windy. Wait. You're going to burn Dad's papers?'

'He hasn't been here for twenty years.'

'I think you should ask him,' said my sister. 'I really do. You should go and see him, tell him you're staying there, see what he says. You should have done it already.'

There was a long silence.

'Honestly,' said my sister.

'Do you know where he is?' I said.

'He's probably at work.'

'In the pub?'

'Yep.'

I parked my car outside the pub in Dad's village, which was the third village in a triangle that consisted of Dad's village, my sister's village and the village that had the shed in it. From inside the car, I could see Dad's shadow moving around on the other side of the frosted glass in the pub window.

Dad had the stocky build and boxy chest of a fighter. His maternal ancestors escaped to Liverpool from Ireland during the potato famine, when a million others starved to death.

Dad's mum, my nainy, was working in a munitions factory in Liverpool by the time she was twelve years old. When the house she lived in with her parents, brother, and three sisters, was bombed, the family scattered. Nobody knew who was alive or dead. It was years before they found each other. Nainy ended up in Wales, where she met Taidy. (Nainy and Taidy are Welsh for grandmother and grandfather). Taidy, who spoke Welsh as his first language, had just enough English to propose to Nainy, and they eventually had Dad, who was their only child.

Taidy worked as a builder and a lorry driver, until he fell into a vat of boiling tar, spent a year in hospital, and never worked again. Dad was bright enough to go to grammar school, but he flunked his A levels, probably because Taidy was in hospital. By the time he was twenty, Dad was married and had a child. When I was very little, Nainy and Taidy ran a working men's club in Llandudno. There was an ancient clanging elevator and the air was thick with Welsh and smoke. Nainy, who worked behind the bar, was the only woman. My sister and I used to sit on the arm of Taidy's chair, rolling cigarettes in a silver box with a handle. You put the papers in one bit of the box, and the tobacco in another bit, and turned the handle until a perfectly rolled cigarette popped out.

Nainy and Taidy were both buried in unmarked graves (headstones are expensive), a few hundred yards away from where I sat in my car outside the pub where Dad was working behind the bar.

I was nervous, but I knew my sister was right. I needed

to talk to Dad about the shed. I needed to know if the bank still owned it and if they were likely to turn up unexpectedly. I needed to weigh up all the available information and then decide whether or not I could get away with living there for a while. And if I decided I couldn't, then I needed to forget about all the things I wanted to do with my life and turn my attention to the problem of how to make £500 a month, plus bills, starting yesterday, and where I was going to sleep during the Easter holidays and for several months over the summer.

I got out of the car and pushed open the heavy pub door and stepped into the musty gloom of the Snug. It smelled of beer and chips and wet dogs. Dad didn't see me at first. I watched him pull a pint of Guinness and wait for it to settle, then he passed an order to the kitchen and muttered to the man who paid for the Guinness, whom I vaguely recognized, although he was old now and leaning on the bar like it was the only thing holding him up. When he noticed me standing there, Dad came out from behind the bar and hugged me. He asked what I wanted to drink and I said Rattler, which is a strong Cornish cider.

'I've left Bristol,' I said, breaking an awkward silence. 'I tried to call you, but the number didn't work.'

'I've got a new number,' he said. 'Vodafone are useless.'

I waited for him to ask me where I was living, but he didn't. There was a match showing on an ancient television screen screwed into the ceiling in the far corner of the room. Everton was playing.

I waited until Everton had scored their first goal and I had drunk two thirds of my pint of Rattler, and accepted that Dad was not going to ask me anything about my life, or what I was doing in the pub in his village when I was supposed to be living in Bristol. I had never been able to work out if he never asked me anything about my life because he wasn't interested, or if it was his way of being polite.

Ever since I went to university, there had been a barrier between us. When it was his turn to pick me up at the end of term, he never came into the halls to meet my friends and their parents. He sat outside in the white Ford Fiesta, drumming his fingers on the steering wheel, impatient and irritable. It was only recently that I had begun to suspect this had less to do with my own inadequacies as a daughter and more to do with the fact that I was the first person in the family to go to university, and the university I went to was so far outside of Dad's comfort zone, it might as well have been on the moon. It was a long way out of my own comfort zone, too. I wanted to make my parents proud, but instead I seemed to have made us all uncomfortable. I had not even managed to turn my good degree into a good career, or any career. In fact, my life looked scarily like theirs had when they were my age. I lived hand to mouth, grafting, worrying, drinking wine on my own and teetering on the edge of depression. The only difference was that I didn't have any children.

'You know the office,' I said, at last.

Dad didn't reply, but I knew he had heard me because he stopped taking glasses out of the dishwasher and placing them on the shelf under the bar, and looked at me. My stomach turned over, because I loved him, but he did not love himself, and his eyes used to be blue like mine, but now they were red with wine and sadness and the effort of forgetting.

'I was wondering about it.' I pushed the thoughts away. 'Like, what happened, and who owns it now?'

The man with the pint of Guinness was listening. I could hear him breathing.

'I do,' Dad said.

I gripped the edge of the bar. The sound of the football game faded into a kind of surging white noise.

'I thought the bank took everything?'

'They did. But they gave the office back.'

'Why?'

Dad reached under the bar and brought out a half-empty bottle of white wine. He filled his glass, which was one of those little round ones you only ever see in pubs. He held the wine in his right hand and stared at the television.

'Dad,' I said. 'Why did they give the office back?'

'Because of your mother.'

'Because of her why?'

'Because they were hassling her and they shouldn't have been.'

'Hassling her how?'

He put his glass down and held the bar with both hands, keeping his arms straight.

'I bought the office in 1985, with a loan. The loan was for seven thousand pounds. Then I went bust, as you know.'

There was a burst of cheering and chanting and singing from the television in the corner of the room. Dad reached under the bar and pulled out a packet of pork scratchings. He opened it and offered me one. I shook my head. He put the packet down on the bar. I stared at the picture of the pig with the big smile and pint of beer. I remembered seeing the same brand of pork scratchings as a child and being troubled by the fact that the pig seemed to be celebrating his own demise. I was too young to understand that the pig was not in control of his image or his destiny. Dad was still talking.

'After I went bust, your mother and I split up, as you know, and after I left, when you were all still living in the house, the bank started ringing up your mother.'

I remembered the phone calls, and the way the bank wrote letters and charged Mum for the letters. My sisters and I would take the phone off the hook because it rang so often. Mum was experiencing a severe clinical depression, with psychotic episodes. Her persistent low mood had flipped into frequent suicidal thoughts. She was locked in a private hell, unable to sleep or function. The doctor prescribed sleeping pills, which she sometimes mixed with alcohol. She would lie in bed with her eyes closed, talking incoherently about things I didn't understand. Once, she made us all hide from the psychiatric nurses until they went away. She was worried about who would look after me and my sisters if she had to go to hospital. Mum had tried so hard to be the perfect mother, to make up for the difficulties in her own childhood. When Dad went bankrupt and their marriage failed, she was exhausted, destitute and completely on her own.

Mum tried as hard as she could to earn money and save the house, but ultimately it was impossible. The foundations of my life, which had seemed so solid, revealed themselves to be as transient as the sand on the west-facing beach. We lived on income support and free school meals. Unable to sleep, Mum would get up in the middle of the night and wander around the unfinished barn conversion that we still lived in, although it was now in negative equity and nobody was paying the mortgage. She seemed to be hallucinating. Exhausted from not sleeping, she'd collapse into bed in the mornings and often stay there all day. I'd sit on the edge of her bed for hours after school, talking to her even when she was asleep. Sometimes I pressed her, to check she was still alive. I blamed her suffering on things I didn't understand: money, God, fate, myself. The memories were like a vice squeezing my skull, making my head hurt. Dad was still talking.

'They said she owed them seventy thousand pounds. They said it was the interest on the loan I took out to buy the office, which was seven thousand pounds. They rang her every day.'

Dad paused to gulp back some of the wine in the little round glass.

'I thought it was terrible, what they were doing, so I wrote to the bank and I wrote to the MP and I wrote to the ombudsman. I wrote lots of letters and I told them your mother wasn't well. "You've had your money back," I said. "You've had the house. You've had everything, and this is tipping her over the edge."'

The room was so quiet, I could practically hear my own heart hammering.

'I wrote and I rang. "I'm not going to give up until you stop harassing my wife," I said. I think she was still my wife. "I've got nothing," I said. "I've got less than nothing. And my wife's got nothing, and we're getting divorced. You'll never get your money back. You've had your money back. You've had the house."'

Dad gazed at the wall behind me. He shook his head. He tapped the fingers of his right hand on the bar.

'"My wife is not well," I told them, "and this could have serious consequences. If anything happens, I'm going to go after you. You've been warned." I think she was still my wife.'

I swallowed. It was difficult. There seemed to be something solid stuck in my throat.

'Well, this went on for weeks, months. Then, one evening, there was a message on the answering machine. "Just ringing to let you know we've had your letter and the loan is written off completely. And we're sorry for any problems you may have endured."'

Dad stopped talking, as though that was the end of the story. I tried to absorb the meaning of it.

'They stopped hassling Mum?'

'They wrote off the loan. The ombudsman said they had acted unlawfully, ringing her up, chasing her for all that money. They sent the deeds back. I've got them somewhere.'

'I found them,' I said. 'I thought they were copies.' I didn't mention that I had almost burned them.

'Oh, right.'

There was another, longer silence.

'I get why they wrote off the loan,' I said, 'but why did they send the deeds back?'

'They were covering themselves, in case . . .'

'In case what?'

'In case your mother . . . She wasn't well, as you know.'

I looked at the floor, the legs of all the bar stools. Gravity was sucking me into the beer-stained carpet. I felt like my internal organs were collapsing.

'So, you do actually own it.'

'I've been meaning to go over there,' he said, as if it had been two weeks, instead of twenty years.

There was more cheering and chanting from the corner of the room. Dad glanced at the screen. 'Penalty,' he said.

Someone scored. The noise of chanting and singing and shouting filled the Snug. I stood up and leaned on the bar, like an old man.

'Can I live there for a bit?' I said, my voice fading into the chanting of the football fans. Everton had won three–nil, which was such an extraordinary thing that Dad seemed to have forgotten I existed.

'Yes!' he said, and punched the air.

Bread

Man is an animal who more than any other can adapt himself to all climates and circumstances.

I held one of the lighters with a picture of a horse on it next to the big pile of cardboard boxes and shredded paper and old files and weeds that was taking up most of the space in the little triangular garden. I had convinced myself the wind had dropped, but as soon as the papers caught, I knew that it hadn't dropped nearly enough. Flames as tall as me leapt towards the overgrown hedge, fingering the dry gorse. I stood with my back to the shed, feeling the heat in the corrugated iron, torn between panic and elation. The fire seemed to be burning up everything I wanted to let go of, all the regrets and failures and losses, all the things I wished I had done and all the things I wished I hadn't done. The future hadn't been written yet. The fact that Dad owned the shed, even through such bizarre and unhappy circumstances, had changed everything.

According to my massive dictionary, the word 'confidence' has its roots in *trust*. To trust, you have to feel safe. To feel safe, you have to believe that your means of survival are guaranteed.

Before enclosure, in rural Britain, ordinary people's means of survival were guaranteed by common land. Villagers had the right to grow food, graze livestock and collect firewood. Over the centuries, these rights have been eroded, and so has the sense of entitlement that went with them. Not only has common land disappeared, but so has public land. Since I was born, ten per cent of the total land in Britain has been sold by the state to private developers. It used to be possible to squat in disused buildings, and such things as squatters' rights. In 2012, squatting was made illegal.

No wonder house prices were going up and up, along with rates of anxiety and depression. If you didn't own property, then you weren't entitled to *anything*. All you could do was hope the people who owned the factories (and the call centres, and the industrial farms, and the department stores, and the landed estates) would pay you enough to satisfy the demands of the people who owned the land and the houses – often the same people.

I felt changed by the knowledge that the miniscule patch of ground beneath my feet belonged to Dad. My parents were more or less destitute by the time I settled into my tiny room in the red-brick Cambridge college that was supposed to guarantee my future. I struggled to find my future. Instead, I made a lot of mistakes, took a lot of wrong turns and ended up very lost. I did not have the kind of safety net that adjusts for wrong turns and wasted years. My wrong turns and wasted years were permanent. The flames were shrinking. The fire had run out of fuel. All that was left of Dad's life's work was a pile of glowing embers. And the shed.

The fact that Dad owned the shed did not mean that living in it was legal. I was reminded of this when I walked to the stall opposite the duck pond to buy potatoes to cook on the remains of the fire. The stall, which had an honesty box, was operated by one of the people who lived in the concrete bungalows. It sold eggs and vegetables from local farms. The old lady who lived in the house directly opposite the stall was standing in her conservatory, watching me. I had bare feet and sooty hands. I probably had soot on my face. I must have looked awful, possibly even frightening. I lifted my arm and waved. I smiled. I tried as hard as I could to look normal and not in any way threatening, but she didn't smile back.

I bought a bag of potatoes from the stall, swapping them for a fifty pence piece. I didn't have any tin foil, so I just put the potatoes in the embers as they were. I would discard the charred skins and eat the middles. I thought about putting one of the turnips in the embers, too, but decided that would be pushing it. Turnips didn't have skins the way potatoes did. While I waited for the potatoes to cook, I sat leaning back against the still-warm shed, drinking the end of a bottle of red wine out of the green plastic cup I'd bought in Jim's Cash and Carry. I would ring the owner of the beige bedsit in the morning. I wasn't going to rent it. I wasn't going to rent anything. I was going to put all my energy and resources into resurrecting the shed. I was going to make it into a home.

I called my sister and told her what Dad had told me.

'Are you sure?' she said. 'It sounds totally far-fetched.'

'That's what he said.'

'Well, then,' she said.

'Don't you believe me?'

'It's hard to believe. Banks don't normally do nice things.'

It *was* hard to believe, and when I asked Mum about it, her version of events was different. According to Mum's memory, the bank was chasing her for interest on a loan Dad took out against the house we lived in. It had nothing to do with the shed. According to Mum, the bank didn't want the shed, because they considered it to be worthless. It's certainly true that, when my parents finally divorced, the shed wasn't included in the divorce settlement and Dad was deemed to have no assets. I had no idea which one of my parents had the most accurate memory, but I decided that the only thing that mattered was that the shed did not belong to the bank. The only people who could evict me were Dad and the council.

'Anyway,' I said to my sister, 'I'm going to fix up the shed and make it really nice and stay in it for now.'

'Good luck with that,' said my sister.

'No, listen. I'm going to make it look really tidy and I'm going to be the perfect neighbour.'

'Is that why you were burning car tyres in the garden?'

'I was not burning car tyres in the garden,' I protested. 'Who told you that?'

'Just people at the coastguard.'

'That is total bullshit.'

'Anyway,' she said, 'I've been meaning to let you know there's a job going in the cafe in the cove.'

'Which cove?'

'Your cove. The one with the toilets.'

'Really?'

The cafe had looked very closed that morning.

'It's half-term next week.'

'How do you know there's a job going?'

'I met the guy who's managing it on a coastguard shout. He's a climber called Justin'

My sister sounded very pleased with herself. I hoped she wasn't matchmaking.

'Do I call the estate?'

'I'd probably start by going down there and finding this climber called Justin.'

'Okay,' I said. 'I'll go first thing tomorrow.'

Justin was much too old for me, even if he did look a lot younger than he actually was. He had ginger hair and tobacco-stained teeth and a smile that was more of a snarl. I liked him. He asked me why I wanted to work in the cafe and I told him I didn't. I said I hated jobs where you had to wear uniforms. I told him it reminded me of being fourteen and working at Land's End every holiday and being shouted at when I told people the prices and explained that Land's End wasn't owned by English Heritage or the National Trust, but by a conglomerate of international oil companies. The uniform meant that people didn't see me as a person, but as an extension of the corporation. I had been paid three pounds fifty an hour (Justin remarked that this was a decent wage, back then) to soak up the abuse meant for oil companies. It took me and my sister an hour to walk to work and we had to clock off for lunch. I said that I thought it was probably this experience that had put me off work altogether. I told him I hated having to work at particular times and I hated having to do what I was told, and I especially hated working with food. I'd had eating disorders when I was younger, and feeding other people when I was hungry sent the wrong message to my subconscious. It made me feel like I didn't deserve to eat, which is how I felt when I became anorexic. Justin went to the counter to serve a man in hiking gear who had just walked into the cafe. I leaned on the chest freezer and thought about pasties.

My eating disorders started when I was sixteen. I think now that starving myself was a way to feel in control, when everything around me seemed to be spiralling out of control. I discovered that being very hungry was a kind of sedative. I became addicted to the calm that was a side effect of my body shutting down. I also became addicted to exercise. As a teenager, I stalked the cliffs around this cafe for hours every day, like an angry warden. Sometimes – but not always

– I'd treat myself to a handful of blackberries. My periods stopped, I grew fur, my breath smelled like rotting vegetables. I was lucky my heart didn't stop. Anorexia was followed by bulimia. When I started to eat again, it was impossible to stop. I ate so much it hurt. I used to buy bags of rotting fruit from the market in town, intended for animals, then panic and throw it all up. This behaviour continued all the way through university.

After university, I discovered I had a talent for getting wasted, and swapped bingeing for drugs. Recreational drugs suppressed my appetite and covered up the underlying problems that caused me to starve and binge in the first place. But the positive feelings that came from chemicals were fleeting and the flip side was anxiety and depression, which led me straight back to the eating disorders. When I was stressed or lonely or sad, I still displaced the feelings on to food, eating too much or too little, or just worrying about it, wasting my life worrying about looking wrong or being the wrong shape.

Since I was a teenager, the number of people suffering from eating disorders had been rising by about seven per cent every year.[17] Iain Pirie, Associate Professor in Politics and International Studies at Warwick University, argues that it's not just the way women are represented in the media that's helping to fuel this rise (a well-documented problem), but capitalism itself, which has corrupted our relationship with our own bodies and the food that sustains them. Pirie argues that the

cycle of bingeing and purging that characterizes bulimia nervosa is similar to the accelerated and chaotic consumption that
underpins modern culture and is vital for economic growth.[18]
The conflicting expectations placed on our bodies by adver-
tisers – bombarding us with messages that food is a reward
and a compensation (Have a break, have a KitKat), while at the
same time telling us that *not eating* puts us higher on the moral
and social hierarchy – are actually deadly.* Eating so much it
hurts and then throwing it up in a fit of utter self-loathing is
the perfect metaphor for consumerism. There is a fatal conflict
between the needs of the economy, manifested as increasingly
raucous advertising and a fetish for growth, and the needs of
people, animals, and the ecosystems that support us, the planet
we must all call home.

The cafe smelled of pasties. I remembered this exact same
smell of pasties from those epic starvation walks, and how des-
perately I used to want to eat one. I wondered if I had enough
change with me to have one for lunch. They were £3.75.

Justin took a tray of tea outside to the man in hiking gear.

'Where were we?' he said.

'I was ranting,' I said, and he snarled.

'Feel free.'

'Working in the cafe will piss me off,' I said, 'because I will
be working for the lord and he will be paying me minimum

---

* Anorexia Nervosa has the highest mortality rate of any psychiatric disorder,
according to www.anorexiabulimiacare.org.uk/about/statistics

wage. The lord knows perfectly well that nobody can live on minimum wage because he rents his houses and cottages out for far more than anyone who is being paid minimum wage could possibly afford to pay.'

Justin looked positively thrilled, so I carried on. I explained that, if I was getting paid the minimum, I was only going to do the minimum, and that I actually wanted an interesting, well-paid job that I could do part-time, which would leave plenty of hours to do other things that were more meaningful to me, like writing a book about my experiences busking from Norway to Portugal with my cello. I told him I was sick to death of having to pretend to be enthusiastic about crap jobs. Nobody in their right mind would *want* to spend their precious time running around with trays of pasties and scones and cream and jam, and wiping tables and washing plates and making tea for men in hiking gear.

I felt a great sense of freedom, knowing that the shed did not belong to the bank, and I could live there rent-free, at least for now. This must be what it meant to feel empowered. I could afford to be honest with potential employers. I could afford to walk away if I felt like I was being exploited. I could live on potatoes that fell off the back of the lorries that were ferrying them away to be turned into crisps. The ditches were full of potatoes. The fields were full of spring greens and cabbages. There was sea spinach all over the place and wild apple trees and edible seaweed – not that I ever actually ate seaweed, but I knew it was there.

Justin told me I would only be needed for a few hours at lunchtime, and that, if the weather was bad or if there were no customers, he'd probably have to send me home.

'It could be quite annoying,' he said.

'I have to come here every day, anyway,' I said, 'to use the toilets.'

'You don't have a toilet?'

'I live in the shed at the end of the lane.'

Justin raised his ginger eyebrows.

'So *you* were the one burning car tyres?'

'I was not burning car tyres.'

'I've often wondered about that building,' he said. 'Who owns it?'

'My dad,' I said, proudly.

Justin made us two flat whites. We carried them to the wooden bench at the top of the slipway.

'This cafe never used to serve flat whites,' I said.

'I know. I persuaded them to buy the Gaggia.'

'Good effort,' I said. 'Have you been working here long?'

'No,' he said, 'but I've been working for the estate for years, in one of the pubs opposite the island with the castle on it.'

'Did you hate it?'

'No, it was fun, and the money was better because of tips, but I let them transfer me here because it's peaceful and I'm trying to finish a PhD on the phenomenology of bouldering.'

I looked at him. I wasn't sure whether to admit I didn't know what phenomenology was.

'Anyway,' said Justin. 'The job's yours if you want it.'

I started the following Monday. I served trays of tea and scones to the families who had moved into the empty houses in the cove for half-term. It was strange seeing the place fill up with perfect strangers who all seemed to know each other. Most of the houses and cottages that didn't belong to the lord were used as private holiday houses. Only a handful were lived in. The permanent residents were polite, but the temporary residents behaved as if I didn't exist, which at least meant I didn't have to talk to them. Then half-term ended and the temporary residents left as suddenly as they'd arrived, and the cottages were cleaned and the little soaps were replaced and the laminated sheets of rules and regulations were wiped and the heating was turned off and blinds were drawn and windows once again stared blankly out to sea.

The cafe was dead. I had finished wiping all the surfaces and restocking the fridges, tidying the ice creams and writing new labels for the cakes. I stood leaning against the counter, staring at the sky.

'How's your book coming along?' said Justin, who was sitting on top of the chest freezer with his laptop.

'I can't seem to work out how to start,' I said. 'It's a problem.'

'You could start by starting.'

'It's not that easy,' I said. 'I need a new battery for my laptop. It's expanded and now it doesn't work, and I can't plug the laptop in because I haven't got any electricity.'

'NASA spent huge amounts of money trying to invent a pen that would work in space,' said Justin. 'Meanwhile the Russians realized they already had one. It was called a pencil. Guess who got a man into space first?'

Justin and I spent some of the hours that technically belonged to the lord sitting on the bench at the top of the slipway, drinking flat whites and discussing the problem of phenomenology. As far as I could tell, the problem of phenomenology was that Justin didn't seem to know what it was either, even though he was doing a PhD in it.

'It's the thingness of things, you know?'

'No.'

'György Lukács said it was about making intuition the true source of knowledge.'

I could only vaguely remember who György Lukács was, even though I was pretty sure I'd studied him, which just went to show how pointless most education was, even at the highest level.

'He's a philosopher,' said Justin. 'He said that modern phenomenology is one of the philosophical methods which seeks to rise above both idealism and materialism.'

'Like Tony Blair?'

'What do you mean?'

'A middle way between rampant capitalism and utopian socialism, otherwise known as politics cancelling itself out?'

'Kind of, only completely different. Anyway, it doesn't really matter what the word means. It's a practice-based PhD. That's what phenomenology is. Practice-based.'

'So, what do you actually do, in practice?'

'I climb big rocks in the middle of the night, wearing a head torch, and film myself, so that all you can see is a line of light.'

'Does someone pay you to do that?'

'No. That's why I'm working here. Which reminds me: I'm going to have to send you home now.'

'Fair enough.'

'We haven't had a customer for two days.'

'I know.'

'I might need you on Friday.'

It was Tuesday.

'Okay.'

To show that I didn't blame Justin for sending me home, I suggested he call in after he finished. I promised to give him a tour of the shed and the garden, which I was slowly bringing back from the brink of wilderness.

I left my apron on the hook by the door and walked home the long way, over the cliffs rather than up the lane. I noticed a pair of seagulls engaged in violent sexual activity. The hedges were also engaged in violent sexual activity. The flowers were jostling for attention, sticking their pollen-coated stamen out for the bees to suck. The blackbird on the telegraph wire outside the shed was singing himself into a stupor for the sake of love and home. I boiled an egg I'd bought from the stall for lunch and spent the rest of the afternoon in my garden.

The word 'garden' has the same root as the words 'yard', 'garth', 'girdle' and 'court' – all various kinds of enclosures. The word 'enclosure' is a loaded word in English, summoning up memories of the time when common land was suddenly fenced in by big landowners, leaving peasants like my ancestors excluded from the places they loved and relied on for food and firewood.

> Now this sweet vision of my boyish hours
> Free as spring clouds and wild as summer flowers
> Is faded all – a hope that blossomed free,
> And hath been once, no more shall ever be
> Inclosure came and trampled on the grave
> Of labour's rights and left the poor a slave[19]

I wondered if the national obsession with gardening was a hangover from enclosure. We tended our little gardens with an industry that verged on the obsessive, fencing them in like the landowners had, putting up signs saying *Private* and *Keep Out*. I loved my own little enclosure, and I was also keen for it to be private and for strangers to keep out. I loved that I could do whatever I wanted to it. I could try making things or planting things, and if they didn't work out I could dismantle them or pull them up and start again. I tried to build furniture out of driftwood, then took it apart because it didn't work. I dug beds for vegetables and collected pallets to make decking. I encouraged things I liked, such as lady's bedstraw, and killed things I didn't like, such as nettles. I enjoyed making order out of chaos. My garden was my kingdom and I ruled supreme.

I didn't have a clue what I was doing when it came to growing things. The only gardening experience I'd had was at primary school, where I shared a plot, two feet square, with my best friend. We experimented with growing things from seed and watching them get decimated by slugs, then we moved up to secondary school and discovered that all the cool people played netball. But buried in me somewhere was an instinct for growing things, a sort of cellular memory that I suspect all humans share. It's part of the innate knowledge we're all born with that we like to call common sense. We know that plants need the same things we need: light, water, shelter, food.

I spent most of that afternoon taking stones out of my newly constructed vegetable beds and then working the lumps out of the soil with my fingers, so that, when I planted seeds, the seedlings would find it easy to wriggle up to the light. I had decided to start by planting things I liked to eat and couldn't afford to buy, such as rocket and spinach and sugar snap peas. I had spent three pounds on seeds so far. Time and slugs would determine whether I would have been better off spending it on a plastic bag full of leaves grown under artificial light in an industrial greenhouse, but I was quietly confident. I knew from when I picked sea spinach that it took seconds to gather far more than I could get for three pounds in the supermarket. It was the same with apples and blackberries. History showed that famines tended to be the fault of politics, not nature. Nature was all about excess.

I had especially high hopes for the rocket. I had seen it growing wild on the peninsula, where it had escaped from people's gardens. Same with fennel. I couldn't afford to buy rocket or fennel in Tesco. In fact, supermarkets increasingly seemed to me to be like conceptual art: rooms full of installations about the abstract nature of price and value; how the value of an apple, say, is vastly increased simply because of the fact that it has been encased in plastic and put on a shelf. You could buy blackberries in plastic cartons, about ten for a pound, and then walk outside and see them rotting in the hedges because there were so many even the birds couldn't keep up. I had always believed the story that supermarkets made food cheaper, but recently I'd noticed more and more examples of this being wrong. I could get a litre of milk fresh from the farm for nearly a third less than a litre of milk cost in Tesco. The vegetables on the stall were dirt cheap, possibly because they were dirty and did not come wrapped in plastic. Sometimes, they had even snails on them, although so far I'd only eaten the snails by mistake. My sister had tried cooking snails and slugs and pronounced the results disgusting.

I worked all afternoon preparing the soil for my seeds, and all afternoon the robin followed me around, eating worms.

Someone once told me that robins were the spirits of our ancestors, and that was why they seemed to want to get close to us. I thought it was more likely the robin had figured out that I was really good at digging up worms.

Justin brought five pasties and two loaves of bread.

'I was only going to throw them away,' he said.

I put the bag with the bread and the pasties in it on the floor, next to the cooker. I would have to do something about them before it got dark, or the rats and mice would have a field day – a field night. Having five pasties in my shed made me nervous, and not just because of the rats and mice. I could eat one, the inside of it anyway (pastry was still against my rules, because it contained unknown quantities of things like butter), but I didn't know what I would do with the others. I worried that I would consume them just because they were there.

Justin was the first person who had seen my shed, except for my sister, and she hadn't been there since I'd burned the piles of boxes and their contents. I pointed out the Ansel Adams post-card pinned to the wall behind the camping cooker, knowing he would appreciate it, and the photograph of my yellow van parked beside a Norwegian fjord with my cello on the ground beside it. I showed him my bag of clothes, which I still hadn't got any drawers for, and my stack of records, which I still couldn't play because there wasn't any electricity. I told him the stories that went with the three guitars that were hanging by their necks from the wooden wall on brightly coloured headscarves that used to belong to the more glamorous of my two grandmothers. And that was it.

'A titan of modern minimalism,' said Justin. 'Makes me want to sell my house and throw away all my things and move into a shed.'

'I'll put the kettle on.'

'If I have any more tea, I'll drown,' said Justin. 'I brought beer.'

'Is it cold?'

'Yep.'

'Cold beer and white wine are the only reasons I miss having a fridge.'

'You could get a gas fridge.'

'I could.'

'But you won't.'

'Probably not. I'd have to buy it, and then where would I put it?'

Justin narrowed his eyes.

'You know, with planning permission, this place might be worth something, even such a tiny plot.'

I felt a lurch of fear inside my chest.

'I don't want it to be worth something.'

'Why not?'

'Because, if it's worth something, Dad might try to sell it. He's completely skint, and so is Mum.'

Another lurch. This time it was guilt.

'I like your driftwood beds,' said Justin, changing the subject.

'Thanks.'

'I like it all.'

'Thanks.'

'Seriously, I'm jealous.'

'What's your house like?'

'Complicated and expensive. I can only afford to pay the mortgage if I move in with my mum every summer and rent the house to tourists.'

'My sister does that,' I said. 'Except she's got three kids and a husband and a dog, and they move into a tent.'

'It rather defeats the object of having a house, if you can't afford to live in it,' said Justin, 'but I make nearly as much money in three months, renting my house out, as I do in a whole year of working.'

We opened the beers and drank them outside, sitting on the pallets by the shower tray and the tap. The sparrows must have had their babies, because they were flying between the hedge and the hole in the shed with insects and worms in their beaks, instead of leaves and twigs. Being a sparrow was hard, especially lately. Three quarters of the sparrows in the UK had disappeared since I was born. If it carried on like that, sparrows would soon be an endangered species. You didn't expect sparrows to be endangered. Endangered things were glamorous and foreign and mythical, like polar bears and elephants and albatrosses. Not sparrows. Sparrows were everyday birds, small and brown and ordinary-looking.

It was difficult to even imagine a world without sparrows. I noticed that the sweet peas I'd planted between the pallets and the fence had sprouted into seedlings, some of them were still wearing the husks of their seeds on their heads, like little hats.

I spat on my fingers and started to rub the mud off my knees. Spit-washing was a habit I'd cultivated since moving to the shed and taking up gardening. I'd forgotten that Justin was there.

'Can I ask you a personal question?' he said.

'It depends what it is.'

'Where do you wash?'

I stopped rubbing the mud off my knees.

'There,' I said, pointing at the chipped shower tray.

'You mean, you stand in that and hose yourself down with cold water?'

'That's right,' I said. 'I try to rub the worst of the mud off first, so I don't have to stand there very long.'

'Hold on a minute,' said Justin, and he got up and went to his van, which was parked behind my car, on the other side of the chevrons. I heard the sliding door opening and closing, and then his footsteps on the pallets. He was carrying a giant yellow bucket, like the ones they sell at the builders' merchants for mixing cement in. The bucket had clearly been used for mixing cement. He handed me the bucket.

'Why, thank you,' I said.

'It'll need cleaning.'

'Why are you giving me a bucket?'

'It's a Tubtrug.'

'Why are you giving me a Tubtrug?'

'I thought you could use it as a bath,' he said, proudly.

Architecture

To what end, pray, is so much stone hammered?

The clocks went forward. The schools broke up for Easter. I told the girl who was subletting my room that I wouldn't be needing it back when the three months were up, and I spoke to a nice lady in a call centre in India about reconnecting the shed to the national grid. The Indian lady put me on hold while she searched for me on her system, then she told me the shed didn't exist. I said that it must exist, because I was standing in it. I said that it used to be connected to the national grid, and that I would have had bills to prove it, except I had burned them. The lady asked me to hold the line. Several minutes later, a man, also Indian, asked me if the shed might once have been called Penwith Planning and Design Services.

'Yes!' I said. 'That's me! Penwith Planning and Design Services.'

'Ah,' said the man. 'It looks like there is an outstanding bill to pay.'

The outstanding bill wasn't the only problem, even if it was nearly three hundred pounds. The electricity had been disconnected for such a long time, I was required to get the wiring checked and signed off as safe by a registered electrician. This not only meant paying a registered electrician, but finding a registered electrician who was sympathetic to the fact that I was living illegally in a shed. Also, EDF wouldn't give me any credit, owing to the unpaid bill, which meant I'd have to pay for a whole year's worth of electricity upfront. This would be calculated according to Dad's previous usage. Eventually, they would refund the difference.

'Why don't you get a windmill?' said Justin.

'Too expensive.'

'What about a solar panel?'

'Same.'

'There used to be grants.'

'Not for sheds.'

I had done my research. You needed a proper postcode.

Someone from the church brought a pile of flyers to the cafe. There was a big subtropical garden in the valley where I lived when I was seven. It was going to be open to the public on Easter Monday. All proceeds would go towards repairing the church roof.

'I used to have dens in that garden,' I told Justin. I was studying one of the flyers, looking at the pictures. 'It belonged to my best friend's grandparents. They lived in the house.'

Justin whistled. 'The circles you move in,' he said. 'I've always wanted to see inside that house. Will you go to the opening?'

I shook my head. 'No way.' I hadn't been near the big house and the subtropical garden for decades, even though it was only two miles from the shed. I tried to explain to Justin that I was afraid of how I might feel and who I might bump into. He snarled and said that, in that case, I should definitely go to the opening. It would be a fantastic opportunity to explore the relationship between place and memory. I should take a notebook, he said, and pretend to be Proust. I should treat it as a phenomenological experiment. I reminded him that Proust understood better than anyone that searching for lost time usually ended badly:

Poets claim that we recapture for a moment the self that we were long ago when we enter some house or garden in which we used to live in our youth. But these are most hazardous pilgrimages, which end as often in disappointment as in success.[20]

'Oh, go on,' said Justin. 'Aren't you curious to measure your adult self against your child self?'

'Not really,' I said, but of course I was curious, and I did end up going to the garden opening, even though it was firmly against my better judgement and entirely outside of my comfort zone.

The path through the woods was so familiar, I could have walked it backwards with my eyes closed. When we lived in the valley, we walked to school through those woods, me and my sister, my best friend and her brother. The rope we used to swing on was still hanging from the sycamore tree. There was a big stick tied to the bottom of it. We'd stand on the stick, one foot each side of the rope, and go lurching through the undergrowth like monkeys. I wondered if the rope would still take my weight. I realized it couldn't be the same rope. It was much too new. The old rope would be frayed and rotten. The rope reminded me of the water in a river, the way it was always the same and always different. The rope looked exactly the same, the tree looked exactly the same, the woods looked exactly the same, but time had shifted. Everything was different.

I had a notebook in my backpack, so I could note down my impressions of the relationship between place and memory. I had brought it to please Justin, rather than for my own benefit, but the longer I stood in the woods, gazing at the rope that was and wasn't the same, the more I felt like taking the notebook out and scribbling in it. The relationship between place and memory was fascinating. Both the place and the memories seemed to be distorted by time. Or perhaps it was time that was distorted by memory. The woods were so familiar to all my senses that I recognized them almost the way I recognized my own body; subconsciously, subjectively, instinctively. This familiarity seemed to make time disappear altogether. The place was so dense with meaning, it was like a black hole. Everything seemed to be happening at once, as though past, present and future had collided.

But, as I walked, I realized the woods didn't look exactly the same. They were smaller and tamer, and someone had planted saplings in the meadow where the farmer who chased us with his gun had grown daffodils and gladioli. He'd chased us with his gun because he was afraid of dogs. Our dog was a rescue dog, insecure and noisy. My best friend's dog was a pedigree springer spaniel. One day, my best friend's dog and our dog had sex. It was the first time I had ever seen anything having sex and I remember thinking that our dog did not seem to be enjoying herself. She whimpered and shivered and showed the whites of her eyes.

The memories were coming thick and fast, now. Many of them were about being chased. My best friend and I were chased by geese on our way through the farmyard between the woods and the school, or at least that's what we told the school when we turned up an hour late for lessons. We were chased by the old lady who lived in the cove and hated children. We were chased by my best friend's older brother. We were chased by the people whose gardens we trespassed through. We were chased after we dared each other to go into other people's houses and make it out again without being seen. We built dens all over the valley so that, when we were chased, we had plenty of places to go to ground.

I came out of the woods on to a track. Next to the track was a house that Dad had designed. Even if I didn't remember him designing it, I would have known he had, because of the dormer windows. Windows like that are everywhere in Wales, but, in this village, they're only on the houses Dad designed.

When I was little and I asked my parents what Dad did for a living, they told me he was an artichoke. It fell to my teachers to explain that he was probably an architect. Artichokes were a kind of vegetable, they said, while architects drew pictures of houses that didn't exist. Dad was not, in fact, an architect. He had trained as a civil engineer and worked for the council in Wales, designing roads and bridges. In the evenings, he designed houses for private clients, and eventually he left the council to do this full-time, moving his business to Cornwall when I was five. He did all the structural calculations and often supervised the building work. He had a good brain and he worked hard. He would be in the office at six in the morning and worked until it got dark. He was less effective at charging people properly for the work he did, and making sure they paid him.

It's hard to build a two-storey, five-bedroom house on foundations laid for a bungalow. Dad's parents did low-paid manual jobs and I know he feels more comfortable pulling pints than he did being an architect. The jobs we do and the amount of money we get paid to do them seems to have far more to do with our expectations, the foundations laid in childhood, than it does with our skills or talents. Boris Johnson gets paid a fortune for writing his column in the *Daily Telegraph*, even though there is plenty of hard evidence that Boris Johnson is not very good at journalism: he makes up quotes, fudges the truth and doesn't bother with research.[21] There is no evidence that he feels remotely uncomfortable about the huge sums of money he gets paid for his mistakes and lies. He clearly feels entitled to it.[22] His self-image expects it. Being paid an ordinary wage would not sit right on the foundations of his life. Most of us expect to have as much as our parents. We find it hard to accept less and difficult to hold on to more. It was striking to me how many of my friends from university were doing exactly the same jobs their parents had done. Not similar jobs, but *exactly the same*. No wonder children of unemployed parents often ended up being unemployed themselves.

Viewed from this perspective, it was no wonder that, in spite of my good degree, I lived hand to mouth in a shed, while my former best friend lived in London and was married to a barrister and also owned a farmhouse at the top of this very valley – a second home she and her husband used for holidays. No wonder that our vastly different circumstances had distorted the magical connection we once had, making it more and more difficult for us to remain friends. I still loved her. I still missed her. I treasured my memories of the dens we constructed together and shared as equals. I remembered those years of freedom and innocence, before I absorbed the meaning of money and property, as the happiest years of my life.

I had reached the entrance to the garden. As I paid the fee, I caught a glimpse of the house that was so big it was effectively a stately home. It was too new to actually be a stately home, but it had been built in the style of one, all wings and gables and verandas, stables and tennis courts and vast greenhouses and heavily landscaped gardens. This was the architecture of privilege and power: beauty as statement; scale as status; church-like towers and endless sloping lawns and servants' quarters, where my own ancestors would have lived, if they were lucky.

I was reminded of the way my best friend used to talk about her claims to fame. She had loads of them: ancestors who were famous for this or that reason – poets and explorers and commanders in the Royal Navy. I only had one claim to fame, which was that Taidy's great-uncle was the first person ever to escape from Ruthin Gaol, where he was locked up for poaching. While my best friend's grandfather was commanding the Royal Navy, Taidy was on the beach in Normandy, getting shot at.

I felt my stomach cramping as soon as I passed under the stone arches of the gatehouse. I couldn't tell if it was hunger or fear. I wanted to run away, back to the life I was building for myself in the shed, a whole new life that had nothing to do with the family who built this house and still lived in it. Except that their power and influence, which was linked to their property, meant that I was beholden. I couldn't afford to fall out with them, even if I wanted to. In spite of my stomach cramps, I kept walking up the drive, putting one foot in front of the other, driven by nostalgia and curiosity and a need to under-stand something deep and mysterious that sat like a stone at the bottom of my psyche, affecting the way I felt about myself.

I veered off the drive and followed a half-hidden path into a dense thicket of bamboo. I stood, completely hidden by the bamboo, listening to the sound of the rustling leaves and, behind it, the sound of the stream making its way to the cove. I closed my eyes and I was seven years old again. It was autumn and the air smelled of bonfire smoke and the ground was crunchy with fallen sycamore leaves and around my neck was a pair of binoculars my parents had given me for my birthday. I was looking through the wrong end of the binoculars at my best friend, who was a million miles away, laughing.

'Let's play beelines!' she shouted.

We made a beeline for the cove, crashing through the bamboo and over the stream, climbing over walls and fences, running through people's gardens, crawling through undergrowth (we were still small enough that crawling was often easier than walking), falling into the river and wading down it in our wellies until we finally got to the sea. We took turns spinning each other on the old wooden capstan, a kind of massive cartwheel turned flat, which we used like a giant roundabout. The capstan smelled of tar and ruined our clothes, but we were oblivious to this, oblivious to the noise we were making, shouting at each other in the language the fishermen spoke, which we weren't allowed to use at school: I ain't going to, it don't matter, bugger off. We were oblivious to the boat that was being dragged up the old granite slipway by a metal rope that was attached to the mechanical winch that was the modern version of the old capstan. We were oblivious to the stench of fish that was rising out of the boat and the fact that the river was running red with the blood and guts of a hundred mackerel. Oblivious to the fact that these years of perfect freedom, in a world of elm trees and sparkling rivers, fertile soil and clean air and a sea full of fish, would turn out to be a kind of curse. The years in this valley were the highlight of my childhood – as they would have been of any childhood – and they would cast a long shadow over my life. I would spend much of my adulthood watching the world I loved disappear, grieving, counting the losses one by one, trying to find my way home.

The bamboo rustled again. I could hear voices on the paths. I made my way out of the thicket and wandered around the garden for an hour, herded this way and that by the crowds of strangers who walked slowly and talked loudly, for whom the garden was just a garden, something to do, a way of passing the time.

I was funnelled into a barn where tea was being served. It was noisy and crowded in the barn, but somewhere among the noise I heard the sound of my own name. It was my former best friend's mother, standing behind a trestle table loaded with scones and cakes. She asked me how I was, and if it was true that I was living at the crossroads, in the shed that used to be my dad's office.

'I am,' I said, because I couldn't lie.

'Jolly well done,' said my friend's mother, a little bit too heartily.

I felt vulnerable and self-conscious and wished I'd changed

out of the charity-shop jeans I'd been wearing for weeks because I couldn't be bothered to drive to the launderette. I asked after my friend, and wrote my number down on a napkin so that she could get in touch, if she felt like it, next time she was down.

Then I ran away, or, rather, walked as quickly as it's possible to walk without actually running, back down the driveway and back under the gatehouse and out on to the lane. I headed for the cove. I crept past the house my friend had lived in, where her brother now lived with his wife and their four children. It was a beautiful house with a thatched roof and roses growing around the door and all the way up to what used to be my friend's bedroom window. I had often stood in front of that house, gazing up at that window, calling my friend's name or throwing stones at the glass, like the children did in Enid Blyton books.

The cottage we had lived in was behind my friend's house, tucked into the side of the valley, hidden halfway up a very narrow lane. It was tiny. There was one room upstairs and one room downstairs, and a small extension with a bathroom in it. Me and my big sister slept, top to toe, in a captain's bunk – a single bed like a high platform with cupboards built into it. My little sister slept in a cot. My parents slept on the landing, behind a wooden partition they had put up when we moved in. There was a larder instead of a fridge, and a very old range, which was so ineffective, Mum cooked most things, including Christmas dinner, on a Baby Belling. We rented our tiny cottage from the National Trust, which had been gifted it, along with most of the cove, by my best friend's grandparents. To their credit, they put covenants on the houses and cottages they gifted to the Trust, restricting the amount that could be charged in rent. Recently, those covenants have expired. When the tenant who is currently occupying the cottage we once rented dies or leaves, that cottage will go up for tender. The person who can pay the most will get the lease. The rent will double or triple. Families like ours won't have a chance.

I was surprised at how some of the houses and cottages on the way to the cove had been extended and altered. I had assumed these houses and cottages were listed buildings. We had moved out of our tiny rented cottage because we were not allowed to turn a concrete outhouse into an extra bedroom. The National Trust said making that sort of an alteration would change the character of the valley. It was true that the character of the valley had changed. It wasn't just that some of the cottages had turned into houses and some of the houses had websites instead of names. It was that there were hardly any boats left on the slipway and no refrigerated vans in the turning area waiting to be loaded up with boxes of fish, no blood and guts and fish heads in the stream. The red telephone box was still there, like a relic, but the big fir tree by the old black garage had been cut down and the old black garage had been demolished.

When I got back to the shed, it was evening. The sparrows were lined up on top of the roof, silhouetted against the sky. I didn't go inside. I went into the garden and took my shoes off and stood on the pallets and looked out over the field that backed on to the furthest allotment. The sun seemed to be caught in the branches of the trees that belonged to the patch of wet woodland at the far end of it. According to my sister, the field belonged to a poet, and this was why it was not cultivated like the other fields.

The poet had bought the field and the patch of woodland and the meadow behind it because he wanted to build a wooden cabin. The cabin had been built by local craftsmen, out of wood and other natural materials. Apparently, it was beautiful. Unfortunately, the poet didn't have planning permission. When someone told the council, they made him tear it down. According to my sister, after the cabin was destroyed, the poet and his wife got divorced, and eventually he left Cornwall altogether. On the deeds I found, which turned out not to be copies, the field is marked as Gladys' Orchard.

I climbed over the broken fence that stood between my garden and the nearest allotment, then over the fence that separated the two allotments, then over the wall at the far end of the furthest allotment. I walked the length of the field, enjoying the feel of the rough grass under my bare feet and the honey smell of the lady's bedstraw. The ground got wetter as I made a beeline towards the woodland, until it was so wet, mud was squeezing up through the gaps between my toes. The woodland was dark and silent, full of blackthorn and hawthorn and hazel and willow and gnarled little wind-stunted sycamores, their branches all twisted and knotted together. It was the perfect place for a den. Moss and lichen and ferns were the background colour, knitting the ground and the sky and the trees into a single coherent scene, like a painting. I saw that there were two distinct types of lichen: one was light green and papery, and the other was darker and bristly. When I put my face against the lichen, it felt like a man's beard.

I struggled through the branches and ferns, too big to crawl, trying not to step on brambles or nettles with my bare feet, until the woodland opened out into a small meadow. The only traces of the poet's cabin were a flattened area in the shape of a circle and a small wooden gate lying flat on the ground, almost hidden by the grass that had grown up around it. I climbed over a granite wall and waded through a small river and came out on the long straight tarmac lane that led to the west-facing beach.

I walked back up the lane a little way, towards the shed, and then swung right, into the allotments. I knew the fishermen weren't around, because their cars weren't there and they never came in the evening. I was trespassing. I was enjoying myself. According to my massive dictionary, the word 'trespass' grew out of the Old French *trespasser*, which means to cross over, to go beyond the usual boundaries – the Latin *tre* means beyond. In modern French, the word '*trespasser*' is a euphemism for dying.

The shed was catching the light from the sinking sun and throwing it back into my eyes. I thought about time and Dad and Boris Johnson and my friend's mother and how it sometimes felt that we were doomed by *psychology* to endlessly repeat the patterns laid down for us by our parents. But, if the status quo was determined by psychology as much as by our circumstances, then surely there was a way to go back to the drawing board and change the blueprints laid down for us in childhood. There was such a thing as self-determination. I realized that the shed had already started to alter the way I felt about myself, and the way I responded to things. The fact that I had been able to visit the valley and the garden, bring up all that shame and discomfort, and not now feel the need to get wasted or make myself throw up – that was new.

Furniture

Nobody is so poor he need sit on a pumpkin.

I needed a desk if I was going to write a book. I could see the desk I needed in my mind's eye. It was the top of Dad's old drawing board, with four sturdy driftwood legs holding it up. I had the driftwood to make the legs. Every time I went to the west-facing beach, which was most days, I found some bit of wood or other to drag back to the shed. Some of the bits I had found and dragged back to the shed were solid square posts. They would make perfect table legs. All I had to do was cut them so I had four lengths the same size. Unfortunately, all I had to cut them with was a very old and rusty handsaw that my sister's husband had found in their garage. I could have driven to Penzance and spent some of my wages from the cafe on a nice new saw, but I was too lazy and too impatient. As a result, I spent about ten times longer than I would have done trying to cut the bits of driftwood, and, when I had finally finished, the four lengths were not the same size. They were *close* to the same size, but close to the same size is not the same as actually being the same size. I was so hot and fed up with sawing, I told myself it didn't matter. It did matter, as I would discover when I had finished nailing the legs to the drawing board (screws would have been better, obviously, but I didn't own a drill, or any screws, for that matter).

When I had finished cutting the driftwood legs and nailing the drawing board to them, I discovered two things. The desk would only stand up if it had something to lean against, like a wall, or preferably two walls, and it was too big to fit through the door to the shed. This was a shame, because I had made the desk in the garden. I had to wrest the legs I had just nailed on, at great effort, off again, only to nail them back on once the desk was inside. It was even harder the second time, because the nails were bent now. By the time I had managed to put the desk back together inside the shed, I was so fed up with the whole thing, I really didn't give a shit that the table, desk, whatever it was, didn't stand up on its own. I jammed it into the north-western corner, where it had two walls holding it up, and hoped for the best. As usual, there was a great gulf between what I could see in my mind's eye and the fruit of my labour in the actual physical world, and the gulf was full of crushing disappointment.

Not only was the desk-table a massive failure, but, while I was making it, the postman had come and laughed at me. He made a comment about how women couldn't cut wood, then he pretended to be me cutting wood, sawing his arm through the air, then he handed me a letter from South-West Water, which was a bill. I had to fill in a form, giving the date I had started using the shed again, so they could charge me from that date. The fact that I wasn't going to be charged for twenty years' worth of water usage was a great relief. It was the first time in my life I had been pleased to get a bill. I filled in the form immediately, put it into the pre-paid envelope and put it on the floor by the door, so I would remember to post it. Getting a bill made me feel like a real person. Also, the fact that I now seemed to have an address the postman recognized meant I could order books on Amazon and get them delivered to the shed. It was a milestone. If I hadn't been so pissed off with the desk, I would have felt like high-fiving myself. The address the postman had recognized was not one I recognized. South-West Water had called my shed *The Shop*.

Now that I had a desk, I wanted more furniture. I wanted a kitchen, for instance, and I could see that in my mind's eye, too, probably because I had seen it in real life, in one of the second-hand furniture shops in Penzance. The furniture in those shops was massively overpriced. The kitchen I had seen was just a small shelving unit with no door. In theory, I could have made it. In practice, I definitely couldn't, so I bought it. I also bought a two-hob camping stove, with a grill (the nice men at the tip gave me an empty fifteen-kilo Calor-gas bottle, which saved me £90), a tin opener (opening tins by stabbing them with a penknife is not a great idea), a corkscrew (ditto opening bottles of wine) and five big Tupperware boxes.

The Tupperware was not a luxury purchase. It was the result

of a horrifying food-related incident. In my kitchen area, I kept an open box of muesli. I had been through a phase of eating oatcakes for breakfast, but one morning I decided to have muesli. I shook some of the contents of the box of muesli into a bowl, then screamed and dropped the bowl. There was a mouse *living* in my muesli. It jumped out of the bowl and ran away. I looked closely at the muesli. The little black things that looked like currants were actually mouse droppings. This was war. I opened the big tub of rat poison I had bought in Jim's Cash and Carry on my very first shopping expedition. The box of poison scared me. It was covered in skull-and-crossbones symbols and red triangles and death warnings. I poured poison into cups and empty yoghurt pots and left them in all four corners of the shed. For a few weeks after I'd put the poison down, I kept finding the rotting bodies of dead rodents. It was a grim period, but it didn't last long. Within a month, I had killed them all.

Installing my new kitchen took about five minutes. There was just room for the new camping cooker and my driftwood chopping board on the top of the new cupboard. I arranged my tins and jars and Tupperware on the shelves. I put my vegetables in the piece of fishing net I had used for clothes when I lived in the Iveco, and hung it from a hook I screwed into the side of the cupboard.

Now that I had a kitchen and a desk, I realized I needed storage. I combed the charity shops until I found an old trunk. I took the trunk back to the shed and put everything I owned in it: my tent, my bicycle pump, important letters, my passport, my phone charger, spare toothbrushes, flannels, old wetsuits, cables, plugs, surf wax, soap. I felt very organized. Then I decided I could no longer handle having to rifle through a bin bag full of all my clothes every day, just to find a pair of knickers. I needed a chest of drawers. I couldn't afford one from any of the second-hand furniture shops in Penzance, so I organized my clothes into piles on the floor.

When the Easter holidays ended and Justin cut my hours again, I devoted myself to my minuscule garden. It was amazing how much work such a tiny garden produced. The seeds I'd planted had germinated and turned into seedlings, and the seedlings had a precarious hold on life. They needed protecting from slugs and snails and weeds and birds. I borrowed a strimmer from my brother-in-law and cleared the area in front of the shed so I could park my car there, instead of parking it on the crossroads, where it was too close to the junction and technically causing a traffic offence.

I still sat on the bench at the top of the slipway most mornings and drank flat whites with Justin. The only difference was that now I didn't get paid. Justin said I should reinvent myself as a gardener.

'You could spend your whole life outside,' he said. 'You could wear all your favourite clothes.'

I looked down at my outfit. It was my gardening outfit. Paint-splattered sweater and cut-off jeans and pink towelling visor.

'You'd get paid twice as much for doing people's gardens as you get for working here.'

'You reckon?'

'Well, maybe not twice as much, but more, definitely. Trust me,' said Justin. 'It's easy.'

'How would you know? You hate gardening.'

'Not when it pays twelve pounds an hour.'

'Have you actually been a gardener?'

'Yes,' said Justin, 'but I had to stop because I couldn't stand the clients.'

Twelve pounds an hour sounded very attractive.

'But I don't know what I'm doing,' I said. 'I literally haven't got a clue.'

'It's only gardening. If things die, you blame the weather. If they don't, you take all the credit. If you need lots of work, you say lawns need cutting twice a week. If you can't be bothered to work, you say they only need cutting once every two weeks. The great thing about plants is they grow all by themselves. All gardeners do is tidy up after them. And, if you want to impress people, all you have to do is learn a few Latin names. Don't call montbretia montbretia, call it crocosmia. Call daisies osteospermum.'

'Osteospernum.'

'Osteosper*mum*.'

I knew Justin felt guilty about slashing my hours every time the cafe went quiet. He was trying to help, because he thought I needed money. And he was right. I did need money.

Together, we made little flyers, with my name and telephone number printed on them. Justin typed them up on his computer and printed them out at his house. I decorated them with little pictures of trees and flowers – at least *I* knew they were trees and flowers. I put some of the flyers in the cafe and some in the Costcutter and gave some to my sister to take to the market. Then I went back to the shed, where my home life was still being ruined by what Corbusier had identified as the 'deplorable notion that we must have furniture'.[23]

I made a bench for the garden out of an orange milk-crate and a rectangular piece of plywood I found on the west-facing beach. For some obscure reason, the plywood had *JESUS CARES* painted on it in capitals. Every time I sat on it, I was reminded that *JESUS CARES*. I found it reassuring. I made a chair out of a big yellow buoy with the words *Maria Magdalena* and a number written on it in black permanent marker. My sister and I typed the number into the fishing vessels website, which told us the *Maria Magdalena* came from La Coruña, in Galicia, and that it was missing. When it was stormy outside and I was worried the buoy would blow away, I tied it to the shed. It banged against the corrugated iron, as if it was a fender and my shed was a boat tied to a harbour wall.

As well as the furniture I found and made, I had a handful of items from my previous lives, which I kept because of the stories they told: the stool I used when I went busking around Europe; the stool a friend of my parents made for me when I was born, which had my name carved into it; the penknife

Pierre, the French doctor who dug the Iveco out of a snowdrift in the Alps, gave me when I dropped him off at Malaga airport and almost threw my heart up crying because I knew I'd never see him again; the black daffodil crates I'd had since Jack, the ex who broke my heart, left and I turned to flower picking out of desperation, trying to save up the money to buy the Iveco and run away.

The shed told stories, too. The story of Gladys and her sweet shop. The story of the twins who built the shed, whom I remembered as old men, when they lived in the valley and carved animals out of wood and put them in the windows of their cottage so we would see them when we walked past on our way to school. The story of my pioneering parents making their way south and west from Wales. The story of Dad's business and how it all ended in disaster. The story of how every wreckage contains within it some kind of salvage.

When I wasn't making furniture out of things I found on the beach, I was inventing all sorts of labour-saving devices that had already been invented: hot water that came out of a tap; lights that came on when I pressed a button; a broom that sucked up dirt; a machine for washing clothes; a blender that meant I didn't have to mash up my turnips with a bendy fork from Jim's Cash and Carry.

I could have gone out and bought every single one of these gadgets, of course, and plenty more. I could have got in my car and driven to Penzance and gone to the bank and persuaded them to give me a credit card and gone to Argos and spent hundreds of pounds making my day-to-day life more convenient. This was exactly what good citizens were supposed to do. This was what kept the economy growing and kept the corporations incorporating. I allowed myself to dream of these things, especially when the fork was bending or there was a spider I needed a Hoover to deal with. But I was never seriously tempted to actually spend money on them. Money cost time, and time was the reason I had left Bristol. Time was the reason I was living in the shed. It was May already and I still hadn't sat down at the table I'd made out of Dad's old drawing board, extracted the relevant notebooks from the daffodil crates that lived underneath it and started work, with a pencil, on the book that was haunting me, like a nightmare that wouldn't go away.

There is lots of evidence to suggest that, up to a certain level, money does buy happiness, but once that level has been reached, having more money makes no difference to happiness. It's the same with labour-saving devices. Up to a certain point, they do save labour and free up time. I will never forget the lady I saw in Bolivia, sitting in the mud in her tiny backyard, steadily working her way through a huge pile of dirty washing, with only a bucket and a rudimentary mangle to help her. But labour-saving devices that don't address real necessities often turn out not to be worth the time that's paid for them, or the cost of life to the people who make them, the children in the Congo who pull precious metals out of rocks with their fingernails, the children in sweatshops making clothes for high-street shops. As usual, it all came down to balance, finding the sweet spot, where the losses did not outweigh the gains. It was a sort of natural law, like a table having to have four legs the same length in order to stand up. Technology, furniture, work – they had their place, but their place was a means, not an end. It was the same with houses. They were supposed to facilitate living, not be the point and purpose of life.

I made a cup of tea and drank it on the milk-crate bench, plucking the chords for a song I was writing about living in the shed:

The north wind is behind me and I've planted out my sweet peas,
The money tree is thriving but the best things here are free.

I put the guitar down. I could hear waves breaking on the west-facing beach. I stood up and walked around the garden so I could hear better. The sound of waves breaking on the west-facing beach meant one thing. Surf.

Solitude

We are the subjects of an experiment
that is not a little interesting to me.

I waited until the next morning to go surfing. I got up at first light, which, at that time of year, was half past four, and drove to the beach at the far end of my sister's village, which faced north and was the best beach for surfing. I wanted to have the waves to myself. From the car park on the cliff above the beach, the ocean looked deep and dark and lonely and cold. I shivered. My stomach rumbled. I tried to convince myself it wasn't worth getting in. I decided the waves were unsurfable, closing out instead of peeling, making a mess of white water that would take ages to paddle through. I remembered that my wetsuit was still damp from the last time I'd been surfing. I tried to convince myself the waves were too big and I would drown. Then I tried to convince myself they were too small and I would get bored. It was no use. I was an addict and the sea was my drug. No amount of common sense, cold or hunger made the slightest bit of difference. I would get in because I had to get in, because, if I drove back to the shed without getting in, my whole day would be ruined. I would spend it thinking about what the waves might have been like, knowing I had missed an opportunity to have the whole ocean to myself, knowing, and bitterly regretting, the fact that those particular waves, the ones I had missed, would never break again.

The time between Whitsun and midsummer is the best time to be on the peninsula, the best time to be alive. It gets light at the crack of dawn and stays light until nearly midnight (ten thirty, to be precise). But, at half past four on that late May morning, the sun still hadn't risen high enough to reach the north-facing beaches. Sharp stones pressed into the soles of my feet as I walked down the long flight of steps. The surfboard my friend Chris (who I'm convinced makes surfboards purely for the fun of decorating them – in this case with a bright orange sunrise) made for me was heavy under my right arm. Where the steps reached the sand, I trod on a patch of faded green sea holly and had to sit on a rock to pull the spikes out of my feet. There was a ring of blackened stones a few feet ahead of me, where someone had made a fire. There were piles of boulders at the base of the cliffs, and the boulders got smaller the closer they got to the sea, like a river of stones making its slow journey back to the ocean. Everything seemed to go back to the ocean. The sea was where all life began and all matter – all that mattered – was dissolved. The beach was the liminal zone where solid things were ground into dust, then swallowed by the sea, which in turn melted into the sky. They say drowning is an ecstatic kind of death. When I'm not trying to escape a massive set and freaking out about drowning, I can easily believe it. For me, wading out into the cold and demanding sea is a way of escaping everything, including myself. The ocean is a womb, pre-birth, post-death.

I grew up swimming in the sea, thanks to my mother, but I didn't start surfing until my twenties. I was a mess: anxious, heartbroken, bulimic, hooked on recreational drugs. I smoked and drank and stayed up all night. I started blacking out in nightclubs, having to be carried outside, coming back to consciousness screaming. I had a recurring dream that I had died. My brother-in-law sold me a surfboard, an eight-foot mini mal. Someone gave me a wetsuit. It was a man's wetsuit and it didn't fit. I didn't care. I spent hours every day getting wiped out, near-hypothermic, exhausted. Surfing was a new kind of oblivion and it saved me. Time in the ocean brought me back to myself, pummelled the terror out of my muscles, released the adrenaline that built up inside me like a head of steam.

The surf on the peninsula is consistent, which is to say that it's hardly ever flat. The quality of the waves, on the other hand, is the opposite of consistent. Good waves tend to break on solid surfaces, like submerged tapering reefs, or wrap themselves around points and headlands made of the kind of rock that doesn't scatter spleen-busting boulders everywhere. When they weren't breaking on to boulders, the waves on the peninsula were breaking on to shifting sand. One day the waves would peel, the next day they wouldn't. The tide took six hours to come in and six hours to go out, and the difference between high and low could be more than six metres. This meant that waves could go from peeling to closing out within the space of fifteen minutes. The waves that broke on my local beaches drove me mad with frustration, but, like a lover who blows hot and cold, always promising things and then letting me down, they had me under their spell. The sea was prone to violent mood swings. Often, it would beat me up, knock me over, smack me in the face until I couldn't breathe. It had beaten me up so badly in the past, I'd ended up in hospital. I'd had black eyes and broken toes and a knee so badly twisted I couldn't walk for three months. I always went back for more.

I came to understand that I loved those waves, not in spite of their moods, but *because* they were violent and unpredictable and dangerous. The sea was the one place I knew where humans weren't in control. There were surf shops and surf schools and contests, but the ocean itself was immune to all of this. The ocean never sold out. The ocean didn't even know the meaning of selling out. The ocean was an outlaw, indifferent to our rules and regulations and surf-lifestyle T-shirts and hoodies, oblivious to our needs and desires. The ocean didn't care if I swore at it and it didn't care if I loved it and it didn't care if I drowned. 'To be truly free', wrote the poet and environmental activist Gary Snyder, 'one must take on the basic conditions as they are – painful, impermanent, open, imperfect – and then be grateful for impermanence and the freedom it grants us.'[24]

The ocean was the one place I felt truly free.

Sometimes I didn't even get as far as the waves. I was washed up by the mountains of white water and had to sit on the beach, like a teenager who wasn't picked for netball, watching the boys whooping and getting barrelled. I had started surfing too late to be any good at it. But I was committed, and I tried to be brave, and I was pretty certain I got as much out of my hard-won rides as eleven-time world champion Kelly Slater got out of his. Surfing was a solitary game, or it was for me. For once, I was only ever trying to be better than myself.

I waded out into the deep cold blueness, taking half a dozen waves on the head before there was a lull long enough to allow me to get on my board and start paddling. I enjoyed the sensation of paddling, the feel of the water, the gliding motion. Once I had left the shore break behind – the violent, messy place where the water's energy is transferred on to the land – the surface of the sea turned smooth and glassy, like oil. I could see through it, all the way down to the bottom.

Surfing has a metaphysical dimension – for me, at least. I took comfort in its lessons, which were Zen-like. I noticed that, when I tried too hard, I often messed up and fell off. I strove to be simultaneously relaxed and poised for action. I learned that fear could be positive or negative, depending on how it was channelled, and that panicking was dangerous. I learned to use rip currents like conveyor belts, letting them help me through the white water. I learned to paddle sideways out of the currents, instead of against them, so they didn't drag me out to sea. I learned to line myself up with features on land, so I could remember where I started and compare it to where I was heading and work out whether or not I was going in the right direction. I learned to pay attention to the horizon, so I would know if a big set was coming and have plenty of time to get out of the way. I lived in the moment when I was surfing, which was something I struggled to do in the rest of my life. On land, there was time and the pressure of past and future; all that mattered in the sea was where the next wave was coming from and whether or not I would be able to catch it.

The technical side of surfing – the physical stuff of paddling and popping up and balancing and turning – was difficult, of course. A surfer has to go from lying down to standing up on a breaking wave, with nothing but a slither of fibreglass to balance on, and then has to ride that wave as it rolls in, not just managing not to fall off, but actually riding it, curving with it, carving lines on it, matching human energy so perfectly with the energy of the ocean that the surfer and the wave become one entity and the past and future become an ever-evolving present moment. It was nothing short of miraculous, every single time. It wasn't like learning to do other things, where one half of the relationship, the musical instrument, for example, is stable and inert. Musical instruments present certain technical challenges, which can be overcome, first in theory, and then in practice. Learning to surf, for me at least, was not an effort of will, but an act of surrender, a practice, a form of meditation.

I caught a small wave and rode it towards the beach. As I was paddling back out, the black head of a seal broke the surface of the water, less than ten feet away from me. We stared at each other. His eyes were huge and tragic. He dived and re-emerged in a different place, still less than ten feet away, still staring at me with his doglike eyes. Then he disappeared.

I dived under a wave, pushing the front of my board down with my hands and kicking the back of it down with my right foot, or trying to. I was not very good at duck diving, which meant I spent more time underwater than most surfers. I'd developed the habit of keeping my eyes and mouth open under-water, letting the brine swill around in my mouth. I found it extraordinary that I could let seawater wash in and out of my open mouth without drowning. The reason I didn't drown was the same reason I sometimes got hiccups that went on for ages. The reflex that keeps people hiccupping once they've started is controlled by a nerve that allows the lungs to open enough to take a breath of air and then close off suddenly before gulping water – essential for amphibians, and a hangover from when humans were fish. In our first few weeks in the womb, we all still look like fish. Our eyes are on the sides of our head, our top lip and jaw are like gills on our neck, and our nostrils are on the top of our head. The cleft above our top lip is evidence of the way our faces rearrange themselves in the embryonic stage, according to evolution, so that we're born, not fish, but human.

The water was a clear turquoise, the white sand reflecting the blue of the sky. When I popped up again, I was facing the land and the sun had finally made it over the top of the cliff. The sunlight warmed my face and made my salty eyes sting.

By then, I was really hungry. All I could think about was food. I caught one last wave and then let myself be carried in to shore, lying flat on my board until it scraped the sand. I walked slowly back up the long flight of steps, enjoying the feel of the ground under my feet and the smell of bracken and gorse and the sound of gulls and crows and swallows. I felt clean and relaxed and alive. I also felt smug. I passed half a dozen men in wetsuits walking down the steps with surfboards under their arms. The car park, when I finally reached it, was half full already. Men in hoodies chattered on the grass and on the bench by the picnic table. Vans with signs on them advertising the services of plumbers and electricians and general builders kept arriving and unloading surfers and surfboards. I was torn between irritation that my solitude had been interrupted, and glee that so many fully grown professional adults had woken up on a Monday morning and decided to go to the beach and dress up like seals and mess about in the sea, trying to catch waves, which nobody would ever pay them for, or even know about. It must have been costing the economy billions.

I drove back to the shed and rinsed out my wetsuit and hung it over the rotting fence to dry. I walked barefoot to the stall to buy eggs. On my way back, I stood in the lane, watching the sparrows enjoying a dust bath in the road. It was nine thirty. There was a man walking up the lane towards me with a dog on a lead. I didn't recognize him. When he reached my shed, he stopped.

'Haven't you got anything better to do?' he said.

The dog wagged its tail and sniffed my legs.

I was stunned. Had I heard right?

'I'm sorry?' I said.

The man shook his head. His dog started humping my leg. The man dragged it off and walked away from me, flicking his hand towards my shed as if the very sight of it disgusted him. I looked at my shed through the man's eyes and felt my glee curdle into shame. I was nothing but a dropout. Alone, I could see the treasures that were wrapped up in my failures, the stars shone through the holes in my shelter. Now I saw only the holes.

Solitude is one of the routes to freedom, but it's also the root of fear. By choosing to live in a shed, I had cut myself off from mainstream society. I was on my own. And if there was nobody to follow, then there was nobody to prove that what I was doing was safe, or even possible.

Philanthropy

But all this is very selfish, I have heard
some of my townsmen say.

I assembled my coffee pot and boiled two eggs for breakfast. While I was eating, the postman arrived with two parcels. One contained *A Room of One's Own* by Virginia Woolf, which I had never got around to reading, and the other contained *Walden* by Henry David Thoreau, which was one of those books I felt like I'd read, because I often mentioned it in conversation, but definitely hadn't.

I finished my breakfast and rinsed my plate and cup and left them in the shower tray to dry. I packed my small backpack with a swimming costume, a towel, *Walden*, a pencil, a banana and a flask of tea, made with mint and fennel from my garden. On the way to the west-facing beach, I thought about the man in the lane who had asked me if I had nothing better to do. I ran through all the things I could have said in reply. If only my brain worked quickly enough to think up replies on the spot, instead of long after the moment for them had passed. Presumably, he had been referring to my inactivity, the fact that it was Monday morning and I was just standing there. His words and the way he'd looked at my shed had left me feeling defensive. I had been up since half past four! Admittedly, all I had been doing since half past four was floating around in the sea for no particular reason, staring at seals, but still. I clambered down the wooden ladder and found a comfortable position among the boulders. It wasn't a hot day, but it wasn't cold either. I poured myself a cup of tea and started to read.

Walden was not the easiest book to get into. The sentences were as long as paragraphs. The language was obscure and antiquated. Thoreau was too confident and preachy and *male*. He recommended not drinking coffee or beer. He was so smug, he didn't even drink tea:

> I believe that water is the only drink for a wise man; wine is not so noble a liquor; and think of dashing the hopes of a morning with a cup of warm coffee, or an evening with a dish of tea![25]

On the other hand, there were distinct similarities between Thoreau's life and mine, and I found these similarities validating. I liked the fact that Thoreau also lived in a shed by a pond, for example, even though he was doing it to make a statement, while I was doing it because I seemed to have run out of other options. I knew enough about *Walden* to have anticipated similarities between Thoreau's life and mine. It was why I bought the book, and why I mentioned it in conversation even though I had never read it. What I had not expected was to find the differences between Thoreau's world and mine so poignant.

The world had changed beyond all recognition since Thoreau wrote *Walden*. Compared to what scientists were already calling the sixth mass extinction, not to mention climate breakdown and the increasingly vivid possibility of a nuclear holocaust, Thoreau's concerns seemed heartbreakingly quaint. The noise of trains bothered him, for instance, and he didn't have much respect for the farmer who, after harvesting cranberries with 'an ugly rake, leaving the smooth meadow in a snarl, heedlessly measuring them by the bushel and the dollar only, sells the spoils of the meads to Boston and New York; destined to be *jammed*.'[26]

I was struck, also, by the difference between the way Thoreau seemed to feel about himself and his choices – which were, after all, strikingly similar to mine – and the way I felt. Thoreau would have looked the man with the dog in the eye and told him to stop worrying about making a living and get a life instead. *Simplify, simplify, simplify,* he would have retorted. And then, with a patronising smile, 'the mass of men lead lives of quiet desperation'.[27]

Thoreau would have declared that he was living like a king in his shack, while the man who (presumably) lived in a house, with (probably) a mortgage, was hobbled by the load of possessions he pushed in front of him, 'imprisoned' by his bricks and mortar. Thoreau spent whole days doing literally nothing at all, and was very pleased with himself afterwards. He was convinced that having less meant having more, and that working for the sake of working was absurd.

I moved to another boulder, which had been warming up in the sun, and carried on flicking through the book, looking for encouraging phrases and writing them down in my note-book. It was a relief to have finally found someone who had managed to put my thoughts into words. Thoreau found the 'ceaseless roar and pelting' of long rainstorms soothing rather than terrifying. Far from being ashamed of himself and skulking around, avoiding everyone who might be on the parish council, he insisted that 'he enhanced the value of the land by squatting on it'. Instead of poisoning his rats, he *ate* them *with great relish*. I was so inspired by reading *Walden* that I decided to go back to my shed and sit down at my desk and start my own book, right there and then.

I might have actually done it, too, except that, when I got back to my shed, there was a voicemail waiting for me on my phone. It was from somebody called Melissa, who had an Australian accent and was looking for a gardener. I rang her back and arranged to meet her the following morning at her house, which was the other side of Penzance. Then, instead of digging out my notebooks and starting to think about how to turn them into a book about busking across Europe, I drove to my sister's house to celebrate.

My sister was out, but her house was unlocked. I let myself in, hoping she wouldn't mind. I snuck upstairs and had a shower, then I checked my emails on her laptop. The only email I had was a spam one from the RAC, wondering if people preferred their cars or their partners. There was a link. I clicked on the link. It took me to an empty screen. *There doesn't seem to be anything here*, said the computer. I logged on to Facebook. The first thing I saw was a picture of a rocky beach in the north of Norway, with the logo of a surf shop splashed all over it.

It had taken me months to get to that beach, which was on the far side of some high mountains, on an island in the Arctic Circle. It was one of those places that still represented the possibility of escape, because of its inaccessibility. Nobody I knew had ever been there, or heard of it. There were no shops there, nothing to buy or sell. It was a place I could go to in my mind, when everything got too claustrophobic, when it seemed that everywhere I went someone was trying to rip me off or sell me something. It was terrible that this wild and remote corner of my imagination had also been reduced to an advert.

Without thinking, fired up by reading Thoreau, I reposted the image on my own page with a negative comment about cashing in on nature to sell men's clothing. I called it *metaphorical enclosure*, which was a phrase I stole from Naomi Klein.[28] I forgot that Facebook was a public place, and that some of the people involved with this particular brand were friends of mine. I hurled my negativity into the void and felt a bit better. For about thirty seconds. Then I felt a lot worse. The void was not a void. One of the people involved with the brand, one of my friends, was online. This particular friend lived in London and devoted a lot of time and energy to saving the planet. *We can't all twiddle our thumbs in mighty solitude,* he commented underneath my message, *self-nourishing though that may be.*

There is a widespread assumption that self-nourishment stands in opposition to what Thoreau would have called *philanthropy*. 'Philanthropy', from the Greek *philanthropos*, which means man-loving, is defined in the OED as 'the desire to promote the welfare of others'. I had grown up with this assumption that philanthropy was expressed by *action*, and my friend's comment got me where it stung. I closed the laptop and drove back to the shed. I ran the exchange backwards and forwards in my mind, trying to work out where I actually stood, as opposed to where I stood because I was in the habit of standing there. I did not like to be thought of as lazy and selfish, and I did respect my friend's efforts to save the planet. However, I also agreed with Thoreau, who believed that philanthropy was 'greatly overrated; and it is our selfishness which overrates it'.[29]

There was something increasingly radical in doing nothing, it seemed to me, within a society that had a fetish for being busy. Twiddling one's thumbs in mighty solitude was never going to look like saving the planet, but at least I wasn't causing any harm. 'To the extent that we consume, in our present circumstances, we are guilty,' wrote Wendell Berry. 'To the extent that we guilty consumers are conservationists, we are absurd.'[30] It was Wendell Berry who used the word 'usufruct'* in a critique of capitalism, arguing that, 'the dispossession and privation of some cannot be an acceptable or normal result of the economic activity of others'.[31] It was hard for me to do anything without adding to the dispossession and privation of others. Every time I went anywhere in my car, I was polluting the atmosphere my neighbours needed for their survival, not to mention contributing towards total climate breakdown. Every time I had a cup of coffee, I was helping to justify deforestation.†[32] Every time I logged on to the internet, I was helping to justify the existence of an industry that, on current trends, would be using one fifth of the entire world's electricity and releasing five per cent of its total carbon emissions by 2025.[33] American data centres (places where computers store, process and share information) were going to need as much energy as the whole of Hinkley Point B nuclear power station, the equivalent of 73 billion kilowatt-hours of energy, by 2020.[34] Just imagine the reduction in carbon emissions if everyone in the whole world spent half an hour a day twiddling their thumbs.

As for the solitude part, well, it's a principle of permaculture that most real change starts at the edges and works its way into the centre, while the centre remains committed to upholding

---

* From Latin *usus*: use, and *fructus*: profit or enjoyment, without *abusus*: consumption or destruction. Generally, a system whereby one party is granted the right to use the property of another *so long as he does not cause harm to it.*

† Eleven million hectares of agricultural land worldwide is dedicated to coffee production.

the status quo. Common sense, experience and instinct all told me I had reason, as the French would say, but I still felt guilty. To appease my guilt, I wrote my friend a message apologizing for twiddling my thumbs in mighty solitude while successful go-getting eco-warriors, like him, held exclusive meetings in trendy cafes and brainstormed ways to show the rest of us how to rekindle our connection with nature.

'I'm having a midlife crisis,' I told Justin, later that afternoon.

It was too near bedtime for flat whites, so we were sharing a pot of Earl Grey. The tray with the tea on it was perched between us on the bench at the top of the slipway, where it was in danger of sliding off and smashing on the rocks. Justin peeled his lips back and arranged his tobacco-stained teeth into the snarl that was actually a smile.

'I'm twiddling my thumbs in mighty solitude,' I explained. 'I'm being lazy and selfish and irresponsible. I'm riddled with regret and, at the same time, I know that, if I went back and did it all again, I'd do it all exactly the same way, because I wouldn't know how to do it differently, unless I was a completely different person.'

'That's an existential crisis,' said Justin. 'You can't have a midlife crisis until you're forty-five.'

'How old are you?'

'Fifty-two.'

'Have you had a midlife crisis?'

'It's ongoing.'

'When did it start?'

'When I was forty-five and I realized it wasn't all in front of me anymore. At least half of it, and probably the better half, was behind me.'

'How do you cope?'

'I spend a lot of time twiddling my thumbs in mighty solitude, in the hope that the reason for my existence will suddenly reveal itself. I have discovered it hurts less, in the long run, to embrace my solitude than to try to escape from it. I tell myself that life is a phenomenological event and I'm just observing. That's how I cope with being fifty-two and still working in a cafe for six pounds seventy-five an hour.'

It started to rain. Justin gathered up the tray with the teapot and the jug of milk and the two cups on it. I followed him into the cafe. Justin sat on the fridge and I leaned against the freezer.

'Has it worked? Has the reason for your existence revealed itself to you?'

'Not yet. I live in hope.' Justin snarled again. 'Although, it's probably worth bearing in mind that, when the sophists examined the problem of existence, they found that nothing existed, and that, even if something did exist, then nothing could be known about it, and that, even if something could be known about it, then that knowledge could never be transmitted.'

'Well, that is encouraging.'

'You're welcome.'

'By the way, I've got a client.'

'What kind of client?'

'A *gardening* client. What kind of client do you think? She's called Melissa. She's got a massive house on the south coast, near Penzance. I'm going to see her tomorrow morning.'

'Well done,' said Justin. 'Remember, now, twelve pounds an hour.'

Where I Lived and
What I Lived For

Where I lived was as far off as any region viewed
nightly by astronomers.

Melissa was younger than me. This did not help with my midlife crisis.

'Cut them nice and round,' she said, pointing at two overgrown shrubs, 'like you see in parks?'

The shrubs in question were trying as hard as they could to pass themselves off as trees. They were three times as tall as me and there were birds' nests in their branches. In my opinion, the shrubs looked better as trees, but Melissa was not paying me for my opinion.

Melissa's garden was big enough to actually be a small park. There was a huge lawn and various distinct areas separated by small hedges. There were dozens of overgrown flower beds, a vast terrace with sweeping views of the bay, a swimming pool and even a spare house, a self-contained annexe, which was empty. Briefly, I wondered about the possibility of Mum renting it. She could only get housing benefit for one-bedroom flats or cottages, because of the bedroom tax, but they didn't come up very often. She topped up her rent with a credit card and worried constantly about the repayments. She was on the waiting list for social housing, but so were several thousand others. She should have been getting a state pension, like Dad, but they changed the rules just before she qualified. Dad had a council flat and a pension and a bus pass. Mum was right: it wasn't fair.

Melissa told me the annexe was managed by an agency that dealt with holiday properties. There was more money in holidays than long-term contracts, she explained, as if she'd worked it out all by herself. You could get more out of holidaymakers in six weeks than you could get out of tenants in a whole year, and you didn't have to worry about how to evict them.

The house and garden actually belonged to Melissa's dad, who ran some sort of property-development business in Australia. Melissa didn't elaborate, beyond hinting that the house in Cornwall was an investment that had something to do with tax. She had been living in Dubai before moving to her dad's vast and empty house on the outskirts of Penzance. I had the feeling she preferred being based in Dubai, and that coming to live in her dad's tax investment was a punishment, an exile imposed on her because of something she had done that had gone wrong. But she didn't tell me, and I managed not to ask.

In many ways, Melissa was the perfect client. She didn't want references, or enquire about my previous experience as a gardener. This was a shame, because I had lined my sister up to pretend to be a former client, and I'd got Justin to scribble a glowing testimony. All Melissa asked me was how much I charged. I told her twelve pounds an hour, expecting to have to haggle, but she just said that was fine and asked me when I could start.

I was to spend the first day of my two half-days a week weeding around the swimming pool and mowing the over-grown lawn with a miniature John Deere that lived in a double garage with remote-controlled doors. The lawn was covered in daisies and dandelions and buttercups. I suggested leaving it that way, because the flowers were clearly popular with bees, and bees were crucial to the survival of the human race. Melissa didn't seem particularly concerned about the survival of the human race. She only wanted the garden to look neat and tidy. There were three extra-large tubs of a weedkiller called Roundup in the garage. Roundup is a non-selective herbicide. The active ingredient is glyphosate. Glyphosate doesn't just kill weeds, it kills everything: plants, flowers, animals, bees, butterflies, humans. It makes soil infertile. I tried to explain about glyphosate and the evidence that was mounting up about it causing cancer and destroying ecosystems.[35] Melissa said I should definitely remember to wear gloves and goggles.

We walked past the swimming pool and the infinity pool, which was in a glass room next to the swimming pool. The infinity pool was a coffin-sized pool of water in which you could swim against a fake current. Melissa flicked a switch and the current started up. The infinity pool used *a lot* of electricity, Melissa said. *A lot*. But it was worth it. Swimming was much better than lifting weights.

'There are plenty of currents in the sea,' I muttered. I enjoyed imagining Melissa being swept out to sea by a current. She explained that she couldn't swim in the sea because she didn't like cold water.

Melissa was wearing a grey trouser suit and high heels, even though it was July and twenty degrees Celsius. After she'd finished showing me what to do, she went into the house and sat down at the table in the kitchen, which had expensive views of the bay. She sat there all day, working on her laptop. It was like she wasn't allowed out.

The lawn sloped all the way to the sea. It was visibly shrinking. The cliffs on the south coast were made of mud, not granite, and there were bits of lawn on the rocky beach, torn out of the garden by the tide. I was pleased to see the laws of nature working away, in spite of Melissa's total lack of respect for them. I turned off the mower and went to find her. She was hunched over her computer in the kitchen. I explained about the lawn and the natural laws that were causing it to disappear.

'That's fine,' she said. 'We'll build something.'

Soon after I started working for her, Melissa went away. She left me an electronic key for the garage and a typed list of instructions, starting with the shrubs. I waited until she was safely gone before I unlocked the garage and found the ladder and extracted the bucket full of tools and carried them over to the pair of shrubs. I poured myself a cup of coffee from the flask I'd brought with me and wondered how on earth I was going to make the shrubs nice and round, like you see in parks.

If I had actually been a gardener, I might have owned a hedge trimmer. If I owned a hedge trimmer, it might have actually been possible to get the shrubs nice and round, like you see in parks. I did not see how it was going to be possible with a pair of loppers, but I decided that, for twelve pounds an hour, it had to be worth a try. I balanced the ladder against the nearest shrub and set to work. I lopped away, moving the ladder in a clockwise direction, stepping off every now and then to inspect my handiwork. Pruning an overgrown shrub is a bit like cutting your own hair. It's tempting to cut too much off, and then try to compensate for cutting too much off by cutting even more off, until there is practically no hair left. By the time I had finished, there was practically no shrub left. It was sort of round, but didn't look anything like you see in parks.

I started on the next shrub. I couldn't decide whether to learn from my mistake with the first shrub, and do this one differently, or whether it would be better to make them both look the same. In the end, the decision was made for me. I tried to do it differently, but it ended up looking the same. I folded up the ladder and took a good hard look at the shorn shrubs. Had I killed them? They had been left uncut for so long, the foliage had all been on the ends of the branches. I was not at all sure if what was left would regenerate. Using my fingernail, I scraped the bark on one of the branches. The flesh of the shrub was green. I prayed it would stay that way.

Cutting the shrubs nice and round took so long that, by the time I finished, it was time to go home. I walked past the swimming pool on my way back to the double garage, carrying the ladder and the loppers. The swimming pool reminded me that I needed to wash. Gardening is not the ideal career choice for someone who doesn't have a shower. I considered stripping off and swimming in the pool, but the pool was the kind of green that doesn't arise naturally and I thought it might kill me or strip off my skin or bring me out in boils. Normally, I hosed myself down with cold water in the broken shower tray. Once, and only once, I had boiled a dozen kettles and filled the Tubtrug and tried to have a bath in it. What actually happened was I got stuck in it. My bum had a bath, together with a small section of my midriff, while my arms and legs flailed around in the cold, trying to heave my bum out again. It was exactly what you'd expect to happen if you decided to have a bath in a bucket.

There was a shower in the empty annexe. I could see it through the window. It was cruel, standing there all covered in mud, looking at the shower in the annexe. But I had no way of getting into the annexe and no towel and no soap and, anyway, it was too risky. Melissa could turn up unexpectedly. I was supposed to be a gardener. That was why she was paying me twelve pounds an hour.

Later, when I was looking after the gardens of holiday cottages, or cleaning them, I had no compunction whatsoever about taking showers in the empty houses. Sometimes I showered in them even when I hadn't been working. Sometimes I took advantage of the central heating (which was on anyway) to sit and write. I never felt so much as a flicker of guilt, and, as far as I know, none of my clients ever suspected a thing. But it takes a few years of living without a hot shower or heating to build up to that kind of behaviour.

In the meantime, I decided that the least-worst option was to stop at the nearest beach and swim in the sea. It would get the mud off, and at least I would *feel* clean. The nearest beach faced the island with the castle where the lord lived. I left the car by the side of the road and walked for ten minutes, so I didn't have to pay for the car park. There was nobody in the car park and nobody on the beach. There was a line of swans swimming gracefully from the island towards Penzance. I watched them for a while, putting off the moment when I would have to deliver myself into the cold water.

Gardening was the first job I'd had that I didn't resent doing. I realized it wasn't work that I hated, it was being inside, and having to wear uncomfortable clothes, and having to arrive and depart at times that were dictated by other people. Now that I was a gardener, I worked whenever I felt like it. If the tide meant I could only surf in the afternoon, then I'd work in the morning, and vice versa. When the waves were so good I had to surf all day, I worked in the evening, making a bonfire out of the branches that came off the shrubs and cooking potatoes wrapped in tinfoil.

Gardens belong to the people who work in them far more than they belong to the people who own them. Melissa's garden yielded more to me than it did to her, and this knowledge helped me not to feel envious, in spite of her huge house and multiple hot showers. Melissa couldn't even *see* her garden. What she saw was a two-dimensional painting, flat and lifeless, with random bits of orange in it. Melissa didn't like orange, which meant that I spent hours of my life pulling up crocosmia. Crocosmia (in Cornwall, we call it montbretia) is as hard as hell and positively likes being pulled up, but Melissa could not grasp this basic fact of life. She wanted me to pull the crocosmia up and I did it because she was paying me twelve pounds an hour. I felt sorry for her, because she had so much and got so little out of it, and I knew I would eventually get sacked, because I would not be able to eradicate the colour orange from Melissa's world.

When I wasn't pulling up crocosmia for no good reason, I was mowing the lawn. The third time I mowed it, I stopped halfway through. I cut the engine and took off my ear defenders. Without the ear defenders, the job of mowing the lawn was unbearable because of the constant screaming of the engine. Melissa was still away. I had stopped because it had crossed my mind that nobody except me had actually seen the grass since I last cut it. Which meant I might just as well not have bothered cutting it. In other words, I cut the grass for no other reason or purpose than to get paid for cutting the grass. I was back in my existential crisis.

I climbed down from my yellow seat atop the miniature John Deere, for which Melissa's dad had paid close to thirty thousand pounds (I had looked it up on the internet). Thirty thousand pounds was roughly the amount my little sister and her husband had to raise for the deposit on their small affordable flat. It was enough for a whole house in another country, like Portugal, where the fishermen sang fado in the street and the trees grew oranges the size of a baby's head and every day was summer.

I walked to the end of the lawn, where it was falling into the sea. I climbed down the collapsing bank until I reached the stony beach. The stony beach smelled of death. I walked along the sand until I found the source of the smell, which was the rotting carcass of a bottlenose dolphin. The smell was so bad, I had to hold my nose and breathe through my mouth. The dolphin had either got caught in a net, or lost its way because GPS interfered with its sonar. It was hard not to be affected by the sight of a dead dolphin, especially since I knew from personal experience that dolphins were open-hearted, fun-loving creatures who enjoyed surfing.

I left the dolphin and walked along the beach towards the lord's castle, which was floating on its island in the middle of the bay. It was low tide, which meant the causeway was uncovered. There was a line of people making their way over the causeway to the island. From where I was standing, it looked as if the people were walking on water. I felt a flicker of panic, because I wasn't sure what was real anymore. The people looked like ants. I tried to observe the reality that was in front of my eyes, like Justin said I should. I knew with my intellect that they were people and they were walking on a causeway that was uncovered at low tide, but my own eyes were telling me they were walking on water. This cognitive dissonance, this gap between what I perceived and what I believed, was like a sinkhole opening up in my mind.

What if my whole life was a dream and my dreams were reality?

What if there was no such thing as reality?

What if this thing we'd all invested in so heavily, this world of jobs and banks and the minutiae of daily life, what if it *didn't exist*?

In an effort to quash these troubling thoughts, I forced myself to finish mowing the lawn, then I drove to the beach and went surfing, even though there wasn't any surf. I had a wash, at least, if you can call getting in the sea in a wetsuit washing, and afterwards I sat in the top car park with Chris and Charlie, drinking bottles of beer from the Costcutter and watching the sun go down, and discussing what the banks were doing and what the tides were doing and what the swell was doing and what it all meant in terms of what time we would have to get up in the morning.

Charlie and I had met when we worked together at the backpackers' hostel. We hadn't seen much of each other in the intervening years. First I went away, and then she went away. But now we were both back, rekindling a friendship based on surfing and the fact that we both lived in sheds.

Chris, who had made my orange surfboard, was the twenty-first century, Cornish version of Thoreau. He lived in a Citroën

Relay, and would certainly have eaten fried rats with great relish, just to prove a point. He went to get more beers from the box under his bed. He handed me and Charlie one each and said he hoped the sea was going to go flat.

'Why?'

'I've started this thing,' he said.

'What?'

'I'm paddling around the peninsula on my surfboard.'

'What do you mean?'

'I'm paddling around the peninsula on my surfboard. I've done the first leg already.' He explained that the first leg started at the cove at the bottom of the valley where I lived when I was seven, and ended at the west-facing beach. The second leg was from the west-facing beach and around Land's End to the beach where my sister lived.

'You two should come along,' he said.

'Paddle around Land's End on a surfboard?'

The thought of it horrified me. The currents were visible from the cliffs. My brother-in-law, who was a sailor and a member of the lifeboat crew, said the tides off Land's End ran like rivers. Yachts were always being rescued. There were visible wrecks, caves where dead bodies had been discovered, reefs treacherous enough to warrant a lighthouse. The cliffs were very high and steep; you couldn't clamber out if you got tired. It would be bad enough in a kayak, let alone on a surfboard. I glanced at Charlie, but I knew I couldn't rely on her to back me up. Charlie was dauntless. I had noticed this in the surf. She was the one who took off on the giant close-outs that everyone else was scrambling to avoid. The annoying thing was that she made at least half of them. On big days, I often found myself skulking over to the place everyone called Coward's Corner, opposite the cafe, while she paddled out with the men and caught the biggest wave of the day. Her fearlessness sometimes made me feel brave, and sometimes made me feel like a loser. Either way, I didn't want to paddle around Land's End on a surfboard.

'We'd have to wait for the right conditions,' Chris said. 'It'd need to be completely flat, with no wind. Rising tide.'

I looked out at the huge expanse of water far below us, sucking in and out, murky and forbidding now that the sun had reached the horizon and was about to disappear. We all fell silent to watch it dive under, leaving in its wake a blood-red sky. I shivered.

'I'm in,' said Charlie.

'It's never completely flat, with no wind,' I said.

'Forecast looks good for next week,' Chris said.

The sky was all grey now, apart from a thin slither of red, right above the horizon. It looked like an abstract painting. The year was unravelling, like someone had dropped a reel of cotton and couldn't work out how to wind it back in. Midsummer had been and gone.

'Oh, for God's sake,' I grumbled.

People always assumed I was brave, because I did things that most people wouldn't do, like busking across Europe and sleeping out in the Pyrenees on my own, while thunderclouds crashed into the peaks, splitting the sky into pieces. The truth was that I was scared of everything. The reason I seemed brave was that I was always terrified. Everything brought me out in a sweat. Sleeping on the top of a mountain on my own in a thunderstorm was no worse than ringing around for car insurance. It meant I couldn't always tell if something was actually dangerous.

'You know you want to,' said Chris.

'I don't want to,' I said. 'But I probably fucking will.'

The Ponds

I had come to this pond adventurously, from time
to time, in dark summer nights, with a companion.
But now I had made my home by the shore.

It was the middle of July before there was a high pressure that lasted long enough to turn the sea into a pond and stop the wind. We left the Citroën Relay in the car park by the harbour in my sister's village, where we planned to eventually make landfall, and set off on foot from my shed. It was such strange, hot weather, we decided to wear rash vests and shorts, instead of full wetsuits.

Charlie and I had borrowed longboards, because they were easier to paddle than the boards we used for catching waves. Chris had a board he had made himself, and painted bright green. It was huge and wide, designed for catching small, crowded waves and putting the fear of God into anybody else who was trying to catch them. I could hardly lift it. If it hit me on the head, I'd probably die. The longboard I had borrowed was heavy, too, and almost too wide to fit under my arm. I was tired before we even got to the west-facing beach, and the tide had been coming in for three hours already.

'I hope we're not too late,' said Charlie, standing at the top of the wooden ladder.

I hoped fervently that we were.

'I don't think so,' said Chris, 'but we should get going.'

I stumbled over the boulders after the others, carrying the bulky longboard. Fear made me less sure-footed than usual. I fell over, near the water's edge, where the boulders were wet and covered in slippery green seaweed. The borrowed board made a sickening clatter as it fell on the rocks. There was more seaweed between the wet boulders and the open water, a great mass of slimy writhing blackness that we had to wade through before we could push off and start paddling. Chris went first, then Charlie, then me. It was a few minutes before I noticed that we had drawn a crowd.

The seals were not friendly like the solitary seals that came and observed me from time to time when I was swimming or surfing. When I turned to look at them, the one in front barked and showed his teeth. I understood that we had strayed into their territory. We had broken the rules. We were supposed to stay near the shore, where we lived, maintaining a respectful distance from the caves and pools where they lived. The seals chased us until we rounded the headland, and then they disappeared.

Charlie and Chris were sitting astride their boards, waiting for me, legs dangling in the water. My breath was ragged with adrenaline.

'Did you see those seals?' I said.

'Big buggers, aren't they?' said Chris.

We sat on our boards to rest and get our breath back. I looked at the surface of the water. It was the same water I swam or surfed in every day, but it seemed different. There was more of it, this far out, and the depth made the water darker and more opaque. Now that we had rounded the headland and left the shelter of the bay, the sea wasn't flat anymore, either. There was a light breeze, which ruffled the surface. The ocean pushed against the cliffs, surging and falling, surging and falling.

At first, we stayed close to the cliffs. Our instinct wanted us near dry land, as though we could escape on to it, even though the cliffs were unscalable by all but the most competent climbers. Chris and Charlie were competent climbers. I was terrified of heights. It soon became clear that we would be safer further out, away from the battle zone where the states were changing, where the sea was pushing against the cliffs, trying to wear them away, and the cliffs were pushing back with their bulk and their hardness, defending themselves for as long as possible against their relentless liquid enemy.

The tide was racing in. This helped to propell us forwards, but meant there was no going back. Trying to paddle back the way we had come would be like paddling upstream in a river. The boulders at the base of the cliffs were being systematically drowned by the tide. Instead of boulders, there were whirlpools. Once, when we had stopped paddling to rest our arms, I put my face on the surface of the water and opened my eyes. I saw a black forest of seaweed, full of mysterious darting creatures. I lifted my face and looked at the land. The familiar cliffs looked mountainous. Compared to the mountainous cliffs and the vast, teeming ocean, I was like a caterpillar in the middle of a motorway, tiny and soft and defenceless. I was literally out of my depth. I had no scales or fur or blubber. I had no flippers, only cold hands and tired arms, and nine feet and two inches of fibreglass.

We passed caves and inlets and rock pools I had never seen before, a foreign landscape that had existed all this time, just a few miles away from my shed. Mysterious creatures lived there: hair-like seaweed and limpets and purple sea anemones and other strange sucking creatures that washed in and out with the tide. There were great shoals of jellyfish, so many I couldn't paddle without touching them. Luckily, they didn't seem to be the kind of jellyfish that stung. They were not the normal kind of jellyfish. They looked like alien life forms, transparent bags of water with neon pink scribbles in their bellies, and each one slightly different. I still don't know what kind of jellyfish they were. They must have been carried in from some even more foreign landscape by the strange weather patterns and the changing currents.

The light bounced off the water and blinded me. I wiped salt from my eyes and looked out to sea, where Charlie was pointing to the dorsal fins of two basking sharks, their massive bodies moving like shadows underwater. I knew the sharks wouldn't hurt me – they had no teeth, only a kind of grill for fil-tering plankton – but the sheer size of them made me nervous.

Basking sharks are the second-biggest fish in the world, after whale sharks. Some basking sharks are twelve meters long. Once, when I was a teenager, I got close enough to a basking shark to touch it. Its skin felt like sandpaper. I loved the fact that nobody knew where they went in the winter. Until 2008, when a female was tagged for eighty-eight days and it was revealed that she swam all the way from the UK to Newfoundland, in Canada, a distance of more than 2000 miles.[36]

There were thick shoals of eels and whitebait and more jellyfish, the standard purple kind, which do sting. There were hundreds of birds – gulls and kittiwakes and fulmars and gannets and shags and cormorants. The birds dived and swam and dried their wings and ignored us. There were rocks that looked like art. I saw faces, eagles, castles, statues, towers.

We had been paddling for about three hours when we finally glimpsed the man-made structures of Land's End. They appeared on the top of one of the empty cliffs like a mirage. There was no time to stop and congratulate ourselves. The tide was about to turn, and this was the hardest part. The breeze stiffened. Gusts were pushing me backwards. Boulders had turned into islands: grass-topped chunks of land that had become untethered and floated away. Hundreds of herring gulls had gathered on the largest of these islands. When they spotted us they screamed.

I followed the others into a kind of roofless tunnel. It was so narrow and shallow, the bottom of my board scraped rocks and so did my hands. After the tunnel, there was a wide and fast-flowing current heading out towards the lighthouse. We paddled across the current, heads down, aiming for the harbour wall. When I looked up, I saw a line of children waiting to jump off. I spotted my nephew, who waved. I waved back, high on relief and exhaustion. I pulled my surfboard up on to the small harbour beach. My niece and some other children were playing hide-and-seek under the lifeboat ramp. Chris and Charlie were talking to my sister, who was sitting on a towel, reading a magazine. I pulled my board up the beach, away from the tide, and started walking towards them. I stopped, briefly, and turned to look at the sea, but it was two-dimensional again, flat and picturesque and familiar.

Visitors

Many a traveler came out of his way to see me
and the inside of my house.

The schools broke up. The fishermen came every day to weed their allotments. The empty houses in the cove were suddenly inhabited. There was more work in the cafe and in Melissa's garden than there were hours to do it in. Shiny black SUVs clogged up the tiny lanes, driven by people who turned red and got cross when they had to reverse. There were lines of cars parked in the road outside the Costcutter. The fridges were always empty. I had to drink warm beer. Visitors stopped their cars on the crossroads and spent ages trying to capture my shed with their expensive cameras. I couldn't understand it at first. My shed was not typical of Cornwall. It wasn't picturesque, like the granite cottages. I decided, in the end, that the shed must have looked like freedom. It was clear, by then, that someone was living in the broken-down building. Someone – me – had managed to escape.

The sudden influx of people was so intense, it felt like the peninsula had been invaded. I mentally rehearsed the propaganda I had grown up with, which was still repeated: tourism was good for Cornwall, we relied on tourism for our jobs and our economy, we ought to be grateful. It was true that I relied on it. I had relied on it since I was eleven, when I sat at the entrance to the car park at the top of the valley for a pound an hour, and then spent all my wages buying lemon sherbets from the shop that was owned by the same people who owned the car park. Tourism was good because there was no alternative. Crap jobs were better than no jobs. It was true that the people who owned the car parks, camp sites, restaurants and holiday cottages made money. But most people involved in tourism did minimum-wage jobs that only lasted for a few months a year, spent a fortune on parking and half their lives driving backwards because the people with the SUVs wouldn't, or couldn't, reverse. It was easier to get planning permission for a holiday home than an actual home, because the council couldn't afford the services they would be required by law to provide for full-time residents.

I knew it was complicated. I was lucky enough to live somewhere that millions of people wanted to visit on holiday. In theory, I wanted them to enjoy themselves. They worked hard and deserved it. In practice, it was infuriating, and it wasn't just the glaring injustice of the fact that, while some people had spare houses, and made a tidy tax-free profit out of them, others slept on the street or struggled to find places they could afford to rent.

The sorts of jobs tourism provided meant the community

was divided along almost feudal lines. There were people who owned property and people who worked for the people who owned property. Often, the owners of holiday houses lived hundreds of miles away. Sometimes they lived in a different country. They relied on locals to make sure their businesses ran smoothly, but very little of the profit found its way back into the community. Some of the people I had worked for in the past, as a cleaner or housekeeper, and would work for in the future as a gardener, I never even met. I was expected to be on call to fix anything that went wrong for the guests, to buy extra tea towels, or help them light the fire if it wouldn't light. The guests spoke to me as if I was a servant. I only existed in so far as I could facilitate their holiday. It was frustrating. I knew there had to be interesting people among the hordes of visitors, people with news from the outside, people I could have talked to and engaged with. But locals and visitors were like oil and water. We didn't mix.

Things came to a head, like they always did, on August bank holiday weekend. Being on the peninsula in August was like living in a pressure cooker. The summer was almost over. Everyone was desperate to get every last drop of pleasure out of their holiday before they had to go back to work. Everyone was driving around in circles in their SUVs, getting stuck, trying to park, shining powerful headlights through my window and into my eyes when I was trying to go to sleep. I decided to sleep outside.

I had spotted a grassy hollow in the middle of a cluster of

large boulders on the end of the headland, above the west-facing beach. It looked like it would make a good bed. The grass was soft and springy and I could curl up in the shelter of a massive lichen-covered boulder and watch seals and cormorants and gulls swimming and fishing, hundreds of feet below me, in one of the wild bays backed by high cliffs I had paddled past a few weeks previously, the one with the caves and tunnels in the back of it that looked to me like the watchful eye sockets of time.

I wanted to fall asleep listening to the sound of the sea, like the seals did. In fact, I wanted to be a seal, or a crow, or even a rabbit. I wanted to be anything but human. I was sick to death of shopping and driving and talking and craving and striving and plastic Costa Coffee cups caught in the hedges, and car-flattened badgers. We caused so much friction with our violent hurrying. I wanted to lie on my back on the surface of the planet and feel comfortable and easy in the world, instead of rushed and tense. I wanted to watch the stars move slowly across the sky, and be reminded of how tiny I was, how brief my life, how beautiful my home. I wanted to wake up with the sun and feel *at* home, connected to the earth, secure.

Living in the shed was good practice for sleeping out. The boundary between inside and outside was fluid. I washed and cleaned my teeth outside. If I needed to pee in the middle of the night, I had to go outside. Swallows sometimes came inside, and so did robins and wrens. The sounds of rain and wind and geese were as loud inside as they were outside. It was the same temperature inside as it was outside. Going from a broken corrugated iron shelter to no shelter at all would not be much of a jump. Or so I thought. In fact, when the right day came – it had to be warm and still and dry, and there had to be a moon – it seemed like such a big jump, I almost bottled it.

The fear was hardwired, like my fear of spiders. It had nothing to do with logic. The rational part of my brain knew that the only predator I could possibly encounter on the headland above the west-facing beach would be one of my own kind with a few screws loose, and that this was so statistically improbable, I was more likely to die by crashing my car into a hedge whilst driving home from my sister's house after drinking a glass of wine. The fear lived in the ancient reptilian part of my brain – the part that caused my body to release adrenaline when it saw a harmless house spider. The old part of my brain thought it wasn't a good idea to sleep out on the cliffs on my own, because I couldn't watch my own back in the dark. Something was bound to leap out from behind one of the shadowy rocks and eat me.

I left the shed just before sunset, carrying a rucksack with my sleeping bag, a flask of tea, a book, a head torch and a packet of oatcakes. I had already cleaned my teeth, and I was wearing my pyjamas. I spread the sleeping bag out on the grass. In an ideal world, I'd have had some sort of mat, like a Therm-a-Rest, to insulate me from the ground. But this was not an ideal world. I did not possess a Therm-a-Rest. I was cold. The moon was yellow. The cliffs were shadowy and terrifying.

I took deep, slow breaths, hoping to trick my reptilian brain into thinking I was safe. There is a Buddhist tenet that says we have nothing to fear because we were never born and we will never die. I repeated this tenet to my reptilian brain. *Yeah, right,* it said. *Tell that to the wolves.* The colour was draining out of the sky, leaving it dark blue, then grey, then black. Suddenly, day was night and the moon was not yellow anymore, but white. Stars and planets were visible. The stars were very still and very silent. No wonder. Some of them had already died. I lay on my grass-clad rock and enjoyed the light the stars had made before they died, way back in the distant past, in all its present flickering glory.

Time was a function of language, of grammar, and language fell apart when you tried to use it to talk about the life and death of stars. How could the stars be dead if their light was still flickering in my eyes? My atoms were made of stardust; my body was seventy per cent water, like the surface of the earth. I was on a monthly cycle, like the moon. I was at home in this place, this world, this galaxy, this universe; it didn't make sense to be afraid. When the collection of atoms that had, for some unknown reason, come together to make my body, fell apart again, they would be free to make other congregations, to become dogs, or rabbits, or gorse. There were plenty of rabbits on the cliffs. Their warrens were visible as holes in the ground. There were hundreds, maybe thousands of little rabbit holes, presumably leading to the tunnels and chambers of an underground rabbit citadel.

What else was beneath the ground I lay on? Immediately under the grass was granite. To my left and right was granite. I was in a pocket of granite. Inside the granite were layers of time. I could see them, glowing in the moonlight. In the context of granite, time existed as horizontal or vertical stripes in the face of the rock. Some ancient rocky remains of human activity had been found on the headland, too, although nobody knew if they were the remains of a house or a church or a fort, or something else altogether, that we modern people couldn't even conceive of. Perhaps constructing mysterious monuments was the ancestors' way of distracting themselves from the terrifying reality of spinning through space at sixty-seven thousand miles an hour on a ball of molten matter, and not being able to get off – in the same way that we distract ourselves with television and the internet. Perhaps their rituals helped them to feel in control, like my ritual of eating only blackberries had, when I was seventeen.

I gazed up at the immensity that was the night sky. The earth's crust was between five and ten kilometres thick. That was less than the distance between where I was lying and Penzance. Underneath the crust was the mantle, which was hot enough that, if you could somehow film it and speed up the footage, the solid-seeming matter would appear to be flowing like a river. Underneath the mantle was the core, where everything was molten. The more you tried to get to the solid truth of things, the more they broke down and changed shape and melted and dissolved.

The air was cool and fresh and, from a certain perspective, a physical thing, made of particles, like water. In his book *The Great Animal Orchestra*, musician and naturalist Bernie Krause explains that 'sound is transmitted as waves of pressure coursing through air'.[37] I didn't need to read Bernie Krause to understand that wind travels over the land in the same way that waves travel over the sea. The gusts of wind arrived in sets, just like waves; each gust was stronger than the one before it, and between the sets of gusts there were lulls. From this perspective, I was like a fish, swimming in water. All night, I would drink from the waves of air that rolled in sets across my face. My body would do this for me while I was sleeping. How, I did not know, still less why. My body was as much of a mystery to me as the molten core of the earth and the dead-yet-still-flickering stars.

Clouds gathered and started putting the stars out. The remaining stars looked like the twinkling lights of sailing boats, navigating a vast ocean of darkness. The moon was a sailing boat, too, rocking and rolling its way through a tumultuous sea.

I woke up to the sound of gulls and the familiar wail of a foghorn called the Runnel Stone, which was also the name of a shallow reef a few miles offshore, made especially dangerous by tidal races and razor-sharp submerged rocks. It was so foggy, I couldn't see the edge of the cliff, or the sea below. I could only hear it, grinding the teeth of the ancient cliffs, boring holes in them, turning the caves into eye sockets, drilling arches, moving boulders around, smashing them against each other, causing them to crumble into sand. What would be left when the sea had finally finished its epic task, when the whole world was sand? That was a good question. What would the sea do then, with all its inexhaustible energy?

I sat with my back against the rock that had sheltered me all night and drank the tea that was in the flask, while the fog lifted, revealing rabbits. There were rabbits everywhere. They came in and out of their holes, like shoppers on a busy high street, pausing to twitch their noses at each other. I noticed there was something wrong with the tea in my flask. There were bits of solid matter floating around in it. The milk must have been off. I drank it anyway. It was warm and wet, and gone-off milk was only curds and whey, which was what cheese and butter were made of. It wouldn't kill me.

Not having a fridge was more inconvenient now that the Costcutter was always running out of cold beer. I should dig myself a cellar, like Thoreau. When Thoreau lived by his pond, the technique of preserving food in ice was only just being developed. There was a description in *Walden* of how men came in winter and dug great blocks of ice out of the frozen pond and put the ice on freight trains bound for Boston, where it was used to preserve things like milk. Fridges didn't exist. Not that Thoreau needed to worry about lumps of snot-like matter in his tea, having liberated himself from the need for anything apart from water. I picked up the flask and shook it vigorously. I emptied the last of the tea into the green plastic cup I'd bought all those months ago in Jim's Cash and Carry. I peered closely at the floating strings of gone-off milk. They looked like snot, but the more I examined them, the more I knew it wasn't snot. It wasn't gone-off milk either. The more I studied the solid particles which had been floating around in my tea, the particles I had been *consuming*, the more convinced – certain – I was that they were actually the partially dissolved remains of a fat brown slug.

Hawking and spitting, I rolled up my wet sleeping bag and put it back in the rucksack with the flask and *Walden*, which I hadn't even opened, and the head torch, which I hadn't turned on. I didn't have any water. I couldn't even rinse my mouth out. I decided to go to the west-facing beach and rinse my mouth out in the stream.

The fog had retreated even more by the time I got down to the west-facing beach. The Runnel Stone was still sounding, and the fog was visible offshore like a low-hanging cloud, but the beach was rinsed with sunlight. It was empty, but there was something different about it. It was covered in cairns. Dozens of pairs of hands had come and gathered up the sea-scattered rocks and pebbles and made little towers out of them.

I had seen cairns like this in lots of the remote and wild and beautiful places I had been. They were at Knivskjellodden, the most northerly point on mainland Europe. They were on the beach in the Arctic Circle I had ranted about on Facebook. They were on the remote coves of the Outer Hebrides. I had never had a problem with them. If anything, I liked them. They seemed to belong in the same category as offerings in a church, tokens of appreciation and respect. That morning, I saw it differently. I felt that the west-facing beach had been tarnished and tamed. The cairns looked less like offerings and more like the urine trails of dogs marking their territory.

I picked up a small rock and aimed it at one of the cairns. I missed. I tried again. I hit the cairn and a couple of rocks fell off. I sat down. I picked up another rock. I threw it at another cairn. I knocked over cairn after cairn. I got so good at it that I managed to hit the foundation stone of the last cairn with enough force that the whole tower collapsed in one go, like a controlled demolition.

Out to sea, gannets were fishing for their breakfast. They flew just above the surface of the water until they saw a fish, then they flew upwards in a straight line, turned in the air and flew vertically down, like an arrow shot out of the sky. Diving gannets can achieve a speed of a hundred kilometres per hour. They have specially developed neck muscles, a kind of sponge at the base of their bill to cushion them against the impact, and special membranes to protect their eyes.

I clambered over the boulders, climbed the wooden steps and walked up the steep part of the track, humming one of my songs:

There's a dream-catcher hanging from the telegraph wire,
and I'm heating up the coffee on a driftwood fire,

monkeys are howling at the monsoon skies,
and hungry dogs are eating giant flies . . .

While I was singing myself up from the beach, my neighbours were coming out of their houses and gathering in the middle of the crossroads. Some of them still wore their dressing gowns. Some of them took photographs of the chevrons, which were completely mangled. Some of them just stood there and gazed at my shed, which was a mess of broken glass and snapped wood.

From where they were standing in the road, my neighbours could see *inside* my shed. There was a hole in it, big enough for a full-grown adult to crawl through. The corrugated iron around the hole was dented and buckled. The upright that had been holding up the corner that faced the pond had broken in half. The roof creaked and sagged. The glass from the top of the door, the window facing the road and the window on the north end lay in shattered heaps in the lane, on the concrete doorstep and in the driftwood bed I had made, but not yet planted. The shed had been shunted backwards on its foundations. The whole structure had moved. The back wall leaned out at an angle. The ridge of the roof was lower than it had been.

The front of the Transporter was all smashed up, too. Miraculously, the engine still functioned. The boy who had been driving the Transporter had only recently passed his test. The neighbours had heard him racing it down the long straight that ended with the chevrons and the ninety-degree bend. He was lucky to be alive, they said to each other, and later to me. If the shed had been an ordinary sort of house, made of bricks or granite, he would have been killed. If I had been in it, I might have been killed too.

The Village

Every man has to learn the points of compass
again as often as he awakes, whether from
sleep or any abstraction.

The church was on the edge of the village, at the end of another long and winding lane. Not that the village had a proper centre. It was less a village and more a haphazard collection of hamlets and farms and coves and cliffs, and the remnants of the Cable and Wireless training centre that had once been its claim to fame, along with the fact that the first ever telecommunications cable linking the UK to the rest of the world landed on the beach near the church. When we were kids, we used to play on the twisted metal cable. It was as fat as a man's wrist. We used it as a tightrope, oblivious to its historical significance.

The church was made of granite boulders cut into square bricks. Some of them had been laid in the twelfth century, but the site had history reaching back much further than that. There was a stone in the graveyard dating back to pre-Christian times. It was a massive, egg-shaped boulder, cracked in two. Apparently, the boulder was the Devil's work and the crack got wider every time there was a thunderstorm. When the crack was wide enough to accommodate a donkey wearing panniers, the world would end. It was already a lot wider than it had been when I came to church as a child. The boulder, the headstones and the granite bricks were all carpeted in lichen. Rooks nested in the square tower, which also housed three massive bells – one, nearly four hundred years old – whose thick ropes dangled down to the floor of the vestry. The ropes would have been perfect for climbing, for circus tricks, for hanging upside down, holding on with one foot, spinning.

I wasn't supposed to be in the vestry. I'd peeked behind the curtain out of curiosity, because the last time I was in this church I'd been a child, and peeking behind the curtain into the vestry had been strictly forbidden. There was nothing special about it, apart from the thick ropes with their frayed ends and colourful weave. There was a motley collection of tea-stained mugs and a very basic electric kettle, the budget kind. There were some hassocks, or cassocks, or vestments – I couldn't remember what they were called: priests' clothing. Purple smocks and black gowns and wide gold sashes, like the ones contestants wore in beauty pageants.

I left the vestry and walked around the small church. It was very quiet – so quiet, the silence felt like an interrogation. The stained-glass windows distorted the light and made it seem as if it was sunny outside, whereas in fact it was grey and looked like rain. I sat down in one of the pews near the front of the church, the one my best friend and her family always sat in. There was a strict hierarchy as to who sat where. Our pew had been right at the back, near the door, jammed up against the back wall, where you could peel the flaking plaster off with your fingernails. The altar had a gaudy, cultish vibe: the golden effigy of Jesus being murdered; the purple carpet for kneeling on when you went to drink His blood and eat the tiny taste-less wafers that were supposed to be His flesh. But, in spite of the strange objects that had been placed in it, and the weight of the silence, the old building worked on me the way I had known instinctively that it would. My heart rate slowed. The panic-stricken voices in my head were finally quiet. I could sit and think and let the inner turmoil settle.

The shock of finding my shed all smashed up and broken was still present in my body. I could feel it in my tense shoul-ders and restless legs. I could feel it in my gut, in the great surges of adrenaline that were released whenever I recalled the sight of my turntables and cello and guitars and records upside down on the floor with my cooker and my gas bottle and most of my books, all mixed up with about half a kilo of lurid green rat poison. The inside of the shed looked like someone had picked it up and shaken it. It was like looking at the aftermath of a violent struggle or a TV murder. Outside was even worse. I'd stood in the middle of the road with my hand over my mouth for ages, just staring, before one of my neighbours came out and asked if I was okay and offered to make me a cup of tea. The kindness of my neighbours was startling. They told me the boy had been racing. They were indignant on my behalf. They handed me a piece of paper with his telephone number scribbled on it and told me to get his insurance details and chase him for compensation. It was as if I really lived there, as if *I* was one of the neighbours, as if I was one of them.

I am Welsh, not Cornish, and the whole time I was growing up, I felt a keen sense of not belonging. Church was the worst. Mum began her religious phase when I was eight. We marched over the fields to the church every Sunday, wearing kilts and blouses and scratchy tights. Dad was brought up to be a Catholic and Mum was brought up to be an atheist, so it was perhaps not surprising we were never fully accepted into the congregation of this Church of England church. Especially since most of the more down-to-earth farmers and fishermen were Methodists and went to chapel. The members of this church's congregation were mostly retired, and their most important religious rituals seemed to be flower-arranging and coffee mornings. There were all sorts of unspoken rules and regulations, and the shame I felt about what I perceived to be my family's transgressions was even more acute because I didn't know what the rules and regulations were.

Then one day, we stopped going to church. Mum said she didn't want us believing that we weren't fit to gather crumbs from under the table. It was soon after that Mum had her first breakdown, falling into a depression so deep, she never fully recovered. For all I know, the congregation prayed for her in church. Most of them I never saw again.

I thought about them sometimes, and, if I saw them driving around the village, I was reminded of the shame and fear and loneliness I used to feel, and how shame and fear and loneliness was what religion meant to me.

When my neighbours had gone back inside their houses for the second time that morning, I started tidying up the mess in the shed. I was numb with shock. My cello was face down on the floor, but it seemed to have survived – the ancient plywood case had finally proved its worth. One of my guitars had a broken neck, though, and the plastic lids on both the turntables were smashed, the phono lead on one of them had been yanked out and the needles were crushed. I would have to take the electrical stuff to someone's house and plug it in to find out the real extent of the damage. Half a dozen records were cracked beyond repair, but most of them seemed okay. It was the shed itself that was the real worry.

I was gathering the records up and putting them back in their boxes when my sister arrived and told me to stop. Using her phone, she took photographs of everything that had been damaged, inside and out. Only after she had taken about a million photographs did she say that I could reinstate the cooker and make us both a cup of coffee.

'You should keep that gas bottle outside,' she said, watching me heave it back to an upright position and check the valve. 'It's dangerous, having it in here.'

'I worry that people will see it and know I'm living here.'

'Everyone knows you're living here.'

I stared at her. 'Do they?' I was shocked.

'It's right on the road, for God's sake. Actually, I'll make the coffee, you call that number.'

I had never in my life been so grateful for my sister's brisk pragmatism. She handed me her phone. 'Go on,' she said. 'Get it over with.'

I dialled the number. My hands were shaking. The boy who'd crashed into my shed answered. I explained who I was and asked for his name and address, and the telephone number of his insurers. I said there was a lot of damage. He said there couldn't be; the shed was knackered. I wanted to tell him I hated him and that he'd ruined my life. Instead, I put the phone on speaker. My sister listened for a few seconds and then said, 'POLICE'. The boy swore. My stomach lurched. He gave me his details.

'Well done,' said my sister. 'Remember, he could have killed someone.'

I kept the phone on speaker and rang the boy's insurers. A robot assured me that my call was very important, and then put me on hold for twenty minutes. I was a nervous wreck. I hate using telephones at the best of times, and this was not the best of times. I felt like my heart was trying to escape my body. It took everything I had just to keep it from flying out of my mouth. The last thing I needed was the cup of strong black coffee my sister put in my hands, but I drank it anyway.

When I explained what had happened, the man on the other

end of the phone said I would be better off claiming on my household insurance.

'I don't have household insurance,' I said. 'It's not a house.'

'What is it, then?'

'It's a shed.'

'STUDIO,' my sister said, loudly.

'Studio,' I repeated. 'It's my studio.'

'And what do you use your studio for, Miss Davies?'

I looked at my sister, who raised one eyebrow.

'Writing and music.'

'And your belongings were damaged in the incident?'

'My belongings, yes. And the shed, *studio*, itself. I think it will need rebuilding.'

My sister nodded vigorously.

'I'll have to arrange for a loss adjuster to meet you at the property,' said the man.

I looked at my sister.

'Okay.'

The man wanted my details. I gave my sister's address. He told me to make a list of everything that was damaged, and said I would need photographs and receipts.

We went outside. I sat on the pallets and my sister sat on the *Jesus Cares* bench.

'What if you'd been in there?' she said. 'Can you imagine? Where were you, anyway?'

'I slept out on the cliffs.'

'Why?'

'I don't know.'

'Weren't you scared?'

'Yes.'

'Why do you do these things?'

'I don't know.'

'What will you do now?'

'I don't know.'

I couldn't stay with my sister. Her house was still rented out to tourists.

'I think I would have been okay, even if I had been here. The end where I sleep is fine.'

'It would have been fucking scary, though. Imagine being woken up by someone crashing a Transporter into your house.'

The tension in my body had to come out somewhere. I laughed so much I got a stitch. I had to lie down.

'You know what?' said my sister, when I finally stopped. 'This might not be such a disaster.'

'How do you work that out?'

'You might get loads of money from the insurance company. You might actually get enough to rebuild it. People would fall over themselves to stay here.'

'What do you mean?'

'If you rented it out.'

'It's not mine to rent out.'

'Well, Dad, then.'

'It would never get planning permission,' I said, trying to keep my voice steady, trying to sound like I didn't really care.

'Dad applied, you know, before he went bankrupt. It was refused.'

'Maybe,' said my sister. 'Has to be worth a try, though.' She narrowed her eyes. 'You've got attached to it, haven't you?' she went on. 'I can't believe you'd let yourself get attached to a building, after everything that happened when we were kids.'

'I'm not attached to it,' I said. But I was lying.

I lay back on the pallets. Above me, a murder of cackling crows flew headlong towards the wet woodland. I thought about what my sister had said and I knew she was right, and I also knew I was going to keep on sleeping in the shed, even if there was a hole in the side big enough for a grown man to crawl through and the roof looked like it was about to fall in. Possession was nine points of the law.

My sister called her friend, who was a boatbuilder. He had a workshop full of old bits of wood and tarpaulins and other bits and pieces we could use to patch the shed up while we waited for the loss adjustor. The boatbuilder was recovering from a broken heart, and my sister said he could do with something to distract him from his loneliness. She wouldn't tell me how old he was. I guessed he was in his fifties, but he could have been ten years older, or ten years younger.

The boatbuilder arrived at lunchtime, with several lengths of rough-looking timber roped to the roof rack of his navy blue Citroën Berlingo van. The first thing he did was walk around the outside of the shed, patting, smoothing, testing the strength of it, like a doctor examining a patient. Then he went inside.

My sister and I followed him. He put a level against the back wall and pushed it slightly with his shoulder. He shook his head.

'I have no idea why this thing is still standing,' he said.

He untied the ropes and pulled out a length of timber, which he jammed in the corner where the post had snapped. The roof stopped creaking. He nailed sheets of ply over the gaps in the door and the windows, where the glass had fallen out. He hammered the corrugated iron where it had crumpled, so that it was less crumpled and the hole was smaller, then he nailed a piece of tarpaulin over the hole. He prodded the ceiling and scratched his head. There were big gaps between the lengths of tongue and groove, where they had moved away from each other. When he prodded the ceiling, dust and debris fell out of the gaps. The roof was collapsing, the boatbuilder said. The edges were pulling away from each other, like someone doing the splits. He went to the van and pulled another piece of timber off the roof rack. He rummaged in the back for bolts. He peeled away some of the tin around the shed door and some of the tongue and groove on the back wall, which was no longer straight, looking for uprights to fix the timber to. He was making a beam, he explained, to pull the walls back together and stop the roof falling in. It took him ages to find the uprights, because there were hardly any of them. He shook his head.

'I honestly don't know why this thing is still standing,' he said, again and again.

By the time the boatbuilder had finished, it was mid-afternoon. My sister had already left. The boatbuilder and I sat in the garden, drinking tea. He was not especially keen to get back to Penzance, where he was in charge of renovating a big house for a man who designed military drones for the government.

'I'd rather live in a shed,' he told me, grinning. 'Who needs three bathrooms?'

'Well, one would be nice,' I said. 'Where *do* you live?'

'I have a cottage, but it's rented out for another two weeks, so right now I'm in my van.'

I looked at the tiny blue Berlingo.

'How long has it been rented out?'

'Ten weeks, so far. It's worth it, though. Pays the mortgage.'

Before he left, I tried to pay the boatbuilder for his time and the timber, but he brushed me away.

'It's only temporary,' he said. 'Wait and see what happens with the insurance company. You can pay me to do it properly then.'

Once the boatbuilder had gone, I tidied up, then I sat on the board bag and drank a cup of tea. I wanted it to feel normal, but it felt dark and strange. There was only one window left with glass in it. I had never thought of being crashed into before. I had felt safe living in the shed, safer than I had ever felt living in houses with stone walls, where the only thing between me and homelessness was money. But the shed wasn't safe. It was flimsy and fragile, perched on the side of the road, on a blind corner. The sound of a car accelerating down the straight made my stomach lurch. There was the sound of a motorbike backfiring, then another car, then the sound of a car slowing down and stopping. I heard people getting out, doors slamming, the voice of a child, as loud and clear as if he'd been inside with me. The child was asking what happened to the little house. His mother said the little house was broken.

'Who lives here?' said the child.

'I don't think anyone *lives* here,' the mother replied.

I left the church and walked over the fields to the house my parents had moved to when I was eleven, the one Dad had designed, the one where my sisters and I had chosen our bedrooms from the plans, the house that was going to be ours, that was going to make us more like the families in church, more like my best friend's family. It was a beautiful house, with five bedrooms and a washbasin in every one of them, and brass taps on the washbasins, and big sofas and a kitchen table big enough for twelve people to sit around. The only problem was we couldn't afford it.

I stood outside the house, gazing at the window that used to be my bedroom window. I remembered a passage in *Walden*, where Thoreau described an episode from his youth when a wooden hut that belonged to one of his neighbours had burned down. The young Thoreau watched it burn, along with half of Concord, and then 'chanced' to walk back to the burned-out hut the following evening. He discovered the only surviving member of the family who built the cabin 'lying on his stomach and looking over the cellar wall at the still smoldering cinders beneath, muttering to himself':

> He gazed into the cellar from all sides and points of view by turns, always lying down to it, as if there was some treasure, which he remembered, concealed between the stones, where there was absolutely nothing but a heap of bricks and ashes.[38]

I could have climbed over the wall into the garden, like I had a hundred times before. It was the day after August bank holiday and the peninsula had emptied out as abruptly as it had filled up six weeks previously. There was nobody around. The house was clearly empty. But there wasn't any point. There was no treasure, nothing but a heap of bricks and ashes.

My phone vibrated in my pocket. It was Charlie. She had driven past my shed and seen what had happened. She wanted to know if I was okay and if I wanted to go fishing and catch a mackerel and cook it on a fire for our dinner. I had never been fishing, did not own any fishing equipment and did not know how to fish, but I was grateful for the chance to put off going home.

I met Charlie at her shed, which was at the end of a bumpy track, followed by a steep footpath, in the same valley I had lived in when I was seven, only further up. Charlie's shed didn't belong to her, which meant she had to pay rent, but, because it had no electricity, and water and gas both had to be carried in, the rent was much lower than it would have been for a house, or even a room in a house. I was slightly jealous of Charlie's shed, which was bigger than mine and nowhere near the road. Being inside it was like being in a tree house. The downside, as she pointed out, was that it was literally held together with gaffer tape. Instead of a beam to stop the roof caving in, there was a ratchet strap. The end of it was tied to a tree to stop the whole thing sliding into the valley.

Charlie's was not the only shed in that part of the valley. There were half a dozen others. Some were lived in, some were empty, some had sprawling extensions, and one was still being built. Apart from the one that was still being built, the sheds had been there so long nobody seemed to care anymore about whether or not they were legal. They were well away from the road, which helped, and, apart from the one that was still being built, they occupied land that belonged to a single family.

The new shed was being built entirely out of pallets, on land that belonged to an estate, similar to the one that owned the cove and the cliffs behind my shed. While we were loading up her little van with the fishing gear, Charlie told me that the people who were building the new shed out of pallets were free men. They had renounced their names, she explained, which meant they couldn't be arrested and they didn't have to get car tax or have driving licences. In practice, she said, they were always being arrested, and all their cars had been towed away because they weren't taxed.

While we were talking about them, one of the free men appeared in the clearing that doubled as a car park for all the people who lived in sheds. He looked ill. Charlie explained later that it was because he had liberated himself from the tyranny of money, which meant he couldn't buy food. She said he subsisted on potatoes and other vegetables he gleaned from the fields (gleaning was legal, so long as you only took what was left over after the crop had been harvested – not that the free men cared about what was and wasn't legal) and drank his own wee.

'Well,' I said. 'It sounds insane. Still, you can't argue with the fact that they've been living for free, for nearly six months, on land that belongs to the estate.'

'Yeah,' said Charlie. 'Maybe we're the ones who are insane. Apart from the wee part, it's sort of logical. Mind you,' she said, 'now that they've liberated themselves from the burden of owning passports, they can't ever go on holiday.'

Charlie and I were always talking about going on holiday. She had all the Stormrider guides and we were always dreaming about surfing left-hand point breaks in Peru, or right-hand point breaks in Morocco, or even just beaches in Portugal. In theory, we were saving up. In practice, we were both permanently skint.

After we had been fishing for two hours and still hadn't caught anything, I told Charlie about a conversation I'd overheard between the two fishermen who had the allotments behind my shed. They couldn't see I was listening, because of a wall of runner beans that had grown ten feet high in the space of a month.

'Mackerel are late this year,' said one of them.

'They were late last year, too,' the other one said.

'Not this late. Went out thirty-six hours and caught four hundred kilos. Hard going. Everyone's panicking.'

'It's those big boats. Those Scottish boats got ninety-five per cent of the quota; handliners got five per cent. It's not right.'

'I've heard they can fit Wembley Stadium in their nets. They can get a thousand tons in one outing.'

Charlie cast another line into the water as she listened. 'At least I don't feel so crap about myself for not catching anything,' she said.

'At least not catching anything is sustainable.' I opened another can of warmish beer. 'Although I am quite hungry.'

I leaned back against a rock and thought about my shed and watched the light getting sucked westwards until it vanished altogether, leaving us in shadow. There was something special about the light in early autumn, the way it seemed to get under the skin of the cliffs, showing the lined beauty of them, the history that had been scarred on to their faces by time and weather and sea, just like time and weather had put lines on my own face. The cliffs made me feel better about growing old.

The sea was picking up the very last of the sun. It seemed to be made out of liquid glitter. The cliffs on each side of the bay were like circling arms. It was so beautiful, it made my heart ache. Bank holiday was over. It was like the morning after a rave. There was rubbish everywhere, and broken glass, and under it all a tangible sense of relief that everyone was still alive and nothing was broken beyond repair. Except maybe it was. I drew my knees up towards my body and rested my chin on them.

Charlie finally caught a mackerel. She reeled it in and unhooked it and held fast to the slippery body while it thrashed around, drowning in the air, fighting for its life.

Instead of bashing it against a rock to stun it, she cut its head off with a penknife. She said it was quicker and more humane. It was certainly messier. It was hard to believe that such a small fish could contain such large quantities of blood. I wondered what happened to all the blood of all the mackerel that was packed into all the tins that ended up in supermarkets, costing about sixty pence each. You'd think it would cost more than that just to deal with the blood, never mind actually catching the fish. A thousand tons of fish meant an awful lot of blood. Where did it all go?

We dived in the sea to wash the blood off, turning the water red. The air had turned chilly and the sea felt warm by contrast, like it often does in September. On our way back along the footpath, we picked wild fennel to season the fish with.

'Your place or mine?' asked Charlie, when we reached her van.

'Mine,' I said, after a moment's hesitation.

We lit a fire in the fire pit, which was a ring of stones I had found when I first cleared the garden. It was a clear, moonless night. I could see the Milky Way. After we had eaten the mackerel, we sat in the garden in silence. Charlie, who never had enough clothes with her, wore my Norwegian jumper. The jumper made me think of Jan Erik, who'd given it to me when I was hanging around in Stavanger, trying to pluck up the courage to start busking north. Jan Erik helped me out when I didn't have enough change for a ferry, then invited me to be part of the crew when he raced his yacht up the fjord. If it wasn't for Jan Erik and his friends I would probably never have made it to the midnight sun. Instead I would have given up and gone home.

I would put Jan Erik in my book, I decided, when I finally started writing it. Jan Erik was an important character. He got me out of a fix. More than that, he restored my faith in human nature. The world was full of kind people. Like my neighbours, who had offered me cups of tea and had made the boy leave his number. Out of all the shocking things that had happened that day, the fact that my neighbours seemed to have accepted me was the most shocking. I had always assumed it was only a matter of time before they called the council to get me evicted, because I wasn't supposed to be there and I didn't belong. But maybe I had been wrong the whole time. Maybe I was supposed to be there. Maybe I did belong.

The Bean Field

I would be glad if all the meadows on the earth were
left in a wild state, if that were the consequence of
man's beginning to redeem himself.

In my dream, there was a tiny brown bird flying in circles just above my face. I opened my eyes. There was still a tiny brown bird flying in circles just above my face. There was a wren trapped inside the shed and it was flying madly around and shitting on my face. When I finally realized what was going on, I sat up and wiped the shit out of my eyes. The wren flew on to the beam the boatbuilder had installed and perched there, watching me. I got up and opened the door, but the wren didn't seem to be in any hurry to leave. I put the kettle on. While I waited for the water to boil and then for my tea to brew, the wren did a thorough investigation of the inside of the shed. It flew into every corner, hopped round the bookshelves, dislodging the detritus I kept collecting when I went for walks: shells and feathers and nice-looking twigs. I realized the wren must have come in through one of the holes made by the crash, and it was scoping the shed out as a possible nesting place for the winter.

The thought of winter made me nervous. Even before the

shed had been crashed into, I had made no plans or preparations. I had saved a bit of money from all the hours I had done in the cafe during the school holidays, but my hours had been cut right back again, now that the holidays were over, and my savings wouldn't last long; the car was due for an MOT and the insurance had almost run out. I thought about the free men, building their cabin out of pallets on land that belonged to the estate. I was as free as I ever had been, but I still wasn't free. Maybe there was no such thing.

I was exhausted, bone-tired and hung-over. It had been nearly midnight when Charlie finally left. She'd kept asking if I was going to be okay, sleeping in the shed, and I'd said yes, of course, but in fact it had been difficult to fall asleep. I'd lain there, watching the tarpaulin flapping where it was tied over the hole, like tiny people were fighting in it. I'd thought about the twisted tongue and groove, and the boarded-up windows, and the broken turntables and snapped guitar. It had all gone round and round in my head, until finally I'd got up and put Jan Erik's jumper on and gone back outside. The embers in the fire pit were still glowing and the Milky Way was still visible, suspended in space and time, although it had moved to a different place in the sky. The birds were sleeping, but the nocturnal creatures were rustling around in the hedge. I listened to my breathing going in and out, and remembered the girl who had given me the ribbons. If I wanted to live life on my own terms, I had to be fearless.

I went back inside the shed and picked up *Walden*, which was made of the sliced flesh of old trees and words that were even older, and I travelled through time and space into Thoreau's world. I'd read somewhere that reading was the cheapest way to travel, and it was true. I stayed in the cabin in the woods on the shores of Walden pond until the brand-new candle burned to nothing, sputtered and went out. When I woke up, it was almost ten and there was a wren flying around just above my face.

The wren finally went outside and I followed it into the garden with my cup of tea. When I reached the pallets, I stopped. There was a pile of runner beans, courgettes and rhubarb by the tap. I sat down on the *Jesus Cares* bench. One of the fishermen must have left the vegetables there for me. I felt a rush of gratitude, not just for the vegetables, but for the gesture, which told me they cared about what had happened to my shed. I looked out over the poet's field. There was something different about that morning, the quality of the light. It was still summer. The air was warm, but it was thinner somehow, as if the boundaries of perception were less defined.

I had been neglecting my garden because of all the hours in the cafe. I discovered that my garden was full of food. I pulled out the worst of the weeds and found that many of the seeds I'd planted in the spring had grown and turned into vegetables. There was a glut of beetroot and kale and spinach, and some tiny muddy carrots with holes gnawed into them. I found potatoes, even though I hadn't planted any potatoes, and there were some ripe blackberries in the hedge. Between the vegetables the fishermen left as a gift and the vegetables I found in my own garden, I hardly needed to go shopping that week.

Three days later, at lunchtime, a man in a suit knocked on the door. He told me he was the loss adjuster who had been assigned to my case by the boy's insurance company. It was his job to make a thorough assessment of the damage and then write a report for the insurance company, in which he would make a recommendation about what, if anything, they should pay out in compensation. He told me he had already done some background research and found out that the building had been empty for about twenty years, and that there was no record of it being used as a studio. He looked at the sleeping bag and the cooker, and then he looked at me.

'Does the building have power, Miss Davies?'

'No.'

'And do you have any evidence that it was structurally sound before the incident?'

'What sort of evidence?'

'Insurance documents, surveys, that sort of thing.'

'No.'

'I believe you were asked to make a list of any damaged possessions.'

'Yes, I did.'

I gave him the list.

'And you have receipts and photographs?'

'The turntables were second-hand. I already emailed photographs.'

The loss adjuster scribbled something in a notebook, then he smiled – a fake, professional smile.

'I'm going to take a few photographs, if you don't mind, Miss Davies, and then I'll leave you to your lunch.'

The loss adjuster was very thorough. He took photographs of everything. Not just the parts of the shed that were damaged in the crash, which I pointed out, along with the temporary repairs the boatbuilder had made, but close-ups of places where the rust had made holes in the corrugated iron, where the door frame was rotten, where the concrete foundations were exposed in all their crumbling glory.

'Does the roof leak?' he said, looking up at the gaps between the boards.

'No. I mean, it probably does *now*. It didn't before the crash.'

'I see.'

He took photographs of the woodworm holes in some of the tongue and groove, and the rotten window frame that soaked up water like a sponge and rained it on to my head while I was asleep. Then he left, promising that the insurance company would be in touch as soon as he'd made his recommendations.

I had trouble eating my lunch. I was anxious about the loss adjuster. I could tell he thought the whole thing was my fault, and I was trying it on. I couldn't see how someone else crashing into my shed could be my fault, but I felt guilty anyway. I worked in the garden until dusk, then I hosed myself down in the shower tray and sat on the *Jesus Cares* bench with a jam jar of wine and my guitar. The sun was setting into the wet woodland, turning the sky pink, orange, then an unearthly red. When the sun had finished setting and it was properly dusk, I thought I saw something white flapping around in the field. I stood on the Jesus Cares bench to get a better look. It was a barn owl. In fact, there were two of them, a pair. They were hunting low to the ground, fluttering silently, like ghosts.

Some people think it's a bad omen to see a barn owl. They call them demon owls or ghost owls or death owls. In fact, it's more the other way round. Humans are bad omens for barn owls. Data on barn owls is unreliable, as no real studies have been undertaken, but there is plenty of anecdotal evidence that their numbers have fallen dramatically in recent years. In 2017, they were listed as on the of the BirdLife International's 'European Birds of Conservation Concern'.[39] That night, though, standing on the Jesus Cares bench, I was blissfully unaware of the desperate plight of barn owls, and especially my own part in it. I was thrilled to see them. I began watching for them every evening at dusk. I was close enough to see the bird's gold-flecked eyes, which were set on the front of its face, like human eyes.

In the days and weeks that followed, I put in as many hours as possible in Melissa's garden, trying to save up money for the winter. There was plenty to do. It was harvest time, and the raised beds I had planted in the spring were overflowing with produce. I was paid twice for tending Melissa's vegetables.

Once in money, for growing them, and again in food, when I ate them. Melissa preferred vegetables that came washed and sliced in plastic bags.

Sometimes, when I was alone in the shed and the evening was stretching out in front of me, I ate so many vegetables it hurt. Eating too much was a way of dampening the anxiety I felt about the shed being broken and winter coming. The origin of 'want' is the Old Norse *vanr*, which means lack. My body had never forgotten what it felt like to be starving. It always wanted more. It wasn't just me. I suspect the urge to go to supermarkets and fill our trollies with food we don't need is related to our hunter-gatherer instinct. Lack is embedded in the human psyche. We have learned to fight each other for what we need. It's hard for our brains to come to terms with the concept of plenty, or even enough.

When I wasn't harvesting food and eating it until my stomach hurt, I was hoarding it. I hoarded anything that would keep, like marrows, which were ten pence each on all the stalls, and apples, from a tree that was growing wild by the side of the road, half a mile from my shed. I'd noticed the tree when it was in blossom, and had tracked its progress ever since, watching the fruit start and get bigger, wondering if the apples were going to be tart and bitter or sweet enough to eat. One evening, on my way back from Melissa's garden, I tasted one. It was tarter than apples in the supermarkets, but sweet enough. It tasted of bonfires and autumn and home. I went back the next day with the car and three tough bags from Lidl. I had to climb the tree to get the apples I wanted, which were the sun-blushed ones at the very ends of the highest branches. I was so greedy for these fat, sun-kissed apples, I risked life and limb for them, clambering out on to branches that were much too thin to hold my weight.

When I got back to the shed, I sorted through the apples one by one, taking out any that had started to rot. I would eat these first, cutting out the rotten parts and adding the rest to my porridge. I wrapped the rest of the apples, hundreds of them, in newspaper and placed them carefully in cardboard boxes. Apples can last for months if you pack them carefully and keep them separate from each other, so one rotten fruit can't ruin all the others.

My sister arrived with my seven-year-old niece while I was in the middle of sorting the apples. It was the first time my niece had seen the inside of my shed, and, at first, she found it frightening. She whimpered and hid behind my sister and said she wanted to go home. But, after we'd been into the garden and sat on the pallets and seen the robin hopping around, eating the crumbs off the plate I'd used for toast that morning, which I had left in the shower tray, she was happy to go back inside and watch me sort the apples and wrap them up in newspaper and put them carefully in the cardboard boxes I'd got from the Costcutter.

My sister made tea for us both and my niece explored the shed, plucking the strings on the guitar that was lying on the board bag and fiddling with my turntables, which were stacked in the corner, waiting to be fixed. She played with the angel that used to sit on top of the Christmas tree when my sister and I were children. Then she came and crouched down beside me and turned my face with both her hands, so I was looking right at her, and said, 'Aunty Catrina, why does your garden smell of wee?'

'Wee is good for flowers,' I told her, truthfully. 'You've seen how big my nettles are!'

'I want a wee,' said my niece, so we went back outside and she had a wee in my garden, chuckling to herself as she did it. My sister and I waited on the pallets with our cups of tea.

'What are you going to do about winter?' said my sister. 'You'll need heating.'

'I don't know,' I said. 'I don't want to think about it.'

'Look!' said my sister, suddenly, pointing at the field, where one of the barn owls had started hunting.

'There's a pair!' I said. 'I see them nearly every day, although not usually this early.'

'It's not a good sign, if they're hunting in the day,' said my sister. 'It means they're struggling to get enough to eat.'

'Oh, no!'

'I'm surprised they've survived this long, with all the poison you've been dishing out.'

'What do you mean?'

'They eat the rats and mice you've poisoned, and it poisons them and they die.'

'Oh my God.'

'Well, they're not dead, are they? So maybe just don't use any more.'

'I won't.'

'You should log your sighting,' said my sister.

She pulled her phone out of her pocket and stared at it, tapping and scrolling. My niece joined us on the pallets.

'Why is your plate in the shower?' she said, and chuckled again.

'Here you go,' said my sister, showing me her phone. 'There's a place to log them on the Barn Owl Trust website.'

'What's a Barn Owl Trust website?' said my niece.

'It's a place where you can find out all about barn owls,' said my sister.

'What's barn owls?'

'Barn owls are a kind of bird,' said my sister. 'A special kind of white bird, with eyes on the front of their face. We just saw one here.'

My sister scanned the field in case the owl was still visible, but there was no sign of it.

'Why are they special?' said my niece.

'They're special because there's not many of them, and because . . .' She looked at her phone. 'Because they hunt with their ears, and that means they can hear more than *any other animal*.'

'I want to go home,' said my niece, grabbing my sister's arm and trying to pull her towards the road. My sister handed me the phone and knelt down to explain to my niece that she wanted to finish her tea first. She told my niece to stand very still and look at the field and see if she could see a barn owl.

'I wonder who's going to buy the field,' my sister said, casually, after she had managed to distract my niece.

'What do you mean?'

'You know it's for sale, right?'

'What?'

'There's an auction in two weeks. The field, the woodland, all of it.'

'You're joking,' I said.

She wasn't joking.

The field and the woodland and the meadow and all the rest of the poet's land – there was more of it than I'd realized – sold at auction two weeks later. I heard on the grapevine that it went for one hundred and fifty thousand pounds.

That evening, instead of the silent, ghostlike barn owls, there was a jeep doing slow laps of the poet's field. I stood on the milk-crate bench, trying to work out who was driving it. The jeep stopped by the woodland and someone got out, then they got back in and drove slowly up the field towards me. Whoever was driving the jeep slowed down at the wall that divided the field from the allotments, which I knew was the best place for looking at my garden and the back of my shed.

I sat back down on the Jesus Cares bench and wished violently that I had been a different sort of person, the sort of person who knew how to make money. The sort of person who knew what they wanted in time to get it, instead of only when it was too late. I could have bought the field and the woodland and kept them for the barn owls. I could have planted trees and had a polytunnel. I could have cut little paths through the wildness so that people could get lost in it. There was so much I could have done if I'd had a different relationship with money. I saw clearly and for the first time that money was power, and that power could be used for good as well as evil. But it was too late. I'd played my cards so badly I didn't even have the power to speak up for the things I loved. I couldn't go to parish council meetings and plead for the barn owls, because I didn't technically live in the parish. All I could do was stand on the sidelines and watch, while everything that mattered to me was sold.

Higher Laws

The greatest gains and values are farthest
from being appreciated.

I left the car at the end of the track and continued on foot across the moor. It was cold and damp. I moved slowly, hands clasped behind my back, staring at the ground as if I'd lost something. I stopped, bent down, pulled a plastic bag out of one of my pockets and put something into it. I stayed down, scanning the patch of close-cropped grass for tiny psychoactive mushrooms, called liberty caps. Usually, if there was one, there were a hundred, or at least another one, leading to another one, leading to a hundred, but not this time. I straightened up and scanned the horizon for other people. As soon as I picked these wild mushrooms, they became illegal. Which was crazy.

It's true that, consumed in large quantities, the mushrooms could be dangerous, or at least traumatic, but it was also true that there was mounting evidence to show that the active ingredient – psilocybin – was helpful in treating depression; unlike tobacco, say, or high-fructose corn syrup, or alcohol, all of which were perfectly legal, in spite of the fact they weren't the slightest bit helpful in treating depression, and could be fatally poisonous to humans.

I had managed to give up most other drugs, but I didn't see the point of giving up mushrooms. I enjoyed being out on the moors, picking them. I enjoyed the fact that I could only eat as many as I could be bothered to find. If I wanted to get high, I had to get down on my hands and knees in the mud first. I liked that they only grew on unsprayed ground and that they literally thrived on bullshit. I liked I liked how, when I was on mushrooms, the things that normally made me cry with frustration – politicians, adverts, farmers – made me cry with laughter instead. I liked how they appeared in wet and dismal places, just at the onset of winter, when crying with laughter was the perfect antidote to the looming darkness.

It was the middle of October. Normally, I would be at work, but Melissa had called that morning to say that her dad was selling the house, so they wouldn't need me anymore and could I please drop off the remote control for the garage. It was sudden, but not completely unexpected. There was less and less to do in the garden as winter approached, and it was clear that neither Melissa nor her dad were especially invested in the property, except insofar as it was an investment. I'd always known it would only be a matter of time before one or both of them decided it wasn't worth paying me. The fact that I had been half expecting it didn't make getting sacked any easier. It wasn't just the sudden loss of income; it was the fact that I had become emotionally involved with Melissa's garden. All those months of tending it, and now I wouldn't even have the chance to say goodbye.

There were other changes happening. The Devil had spat all over the blackberries, turning them mushy and inedible. The cafe had closed for the winter. The swallows were lining up like soldiers on the telegraph wires, training for their long migration. Justin had already migrated, first to Fontainebleau and then to Spain. He was looking for a house cheap enough to buy outright with what was left over from selling his house in Penzance and paying off the mortgage. He was fed up with moving out every summer and living with his mum, and he was fed up with working for the lord, and house prices were so high in Cornwall that selling up and moving abroad was a no-brainer.

The loss adjuster had finally sent his recommendations to the insurance company, and their claims department had sent me a cheque. Two thousand pounds seemed like a fortune, until I rang my sister.

'Is that all?'

'It's loads.'

'It's not loads. We should have got way more than that. They've completely buggered up the building. That's just about enough for a new door and a couple of new windows. Did they say why it's so little?'

I looked at the letter that had come with the cheque.

'No, but it says I can go online and download a pdf of a summary of the loss adjuster's report.'

'What's the address?'

I gave her the website and she typed it into her laptop. I could almost hear her shaking her head.

'They say the building was unoccupied, so there was no loss of activity or income. They say the building had not been maintained. They say the post in the corner broke because it was rotten. They accept that your possessions were damaged and that there was some damage to the building, but they say it was mostly cosmetic.'

'It moved on its *foundations*,' I said.

'They say they're only legally required to replace like for like, and that you have a right of appeal, but that, if you lose, you will have to pay legal fees.'

'What does "like for like" mean?'

'It means they won't give you nice, new windows to replace old, rotten windows.'

'I can't exactly go out and buy old, rotten windows,' I said. 'It was fine, and now it isn't. Surely they have to give me enough money to make it fine again.'

'I don't think that's how loss works,' said my sister, and she was right. It wasn't.

Loss was the sea grinding the teeth of the cliffs until the holes became caves and the caves became arches and the arches looked like they'd been there since the beginning of time. Loss was the gradual chipping away at the landscape of my memory, until I couldn't see what I'd already forgotten. Eventually there would be nothing left.

I had come up to the moors to look for liberty caps and

because I needed space to think, and the shed was too cold and dark for thinking. In a couple of weeks, the clocks would go back and it would get even colder and darker. Tesco had stopped selling household candles, so I had to get them from Lidl. The candles from Lidl were thin and made of a different kind of wax, which didn't last and gave off such a weak light that reading was difficult.

My phone was ringing. I straightened up and pulled it out of my pocket. It was the boatbuilder. He sounded out of breath.

'We've just ripped an old woodburner out of the house,' he said. 'It's seen better days, and it was crap to start with, but it should do the trick for now. Anyway, it's yours, if you want it. Otherwise, it's going to the dump.'

'Of course I want it,' I said.

'If you can come and pick it up today, that would be ideal, before the client changes his mind and decides he wants it.'

'I'll come right now.'

The woodburner was warped and rusty. It needed a new baffle board and new glass in the door and new rope to go around the glass. I needed chimney piping, double skinned where it went through the wooden roof, heat-resistant silicone, fire cement.

On Saturday morning, the boatbuilder drove me to the stove shop in Camborne in his blue Berlingo van. It felt like a holiday, being driven up the A30 and not having to worry about my car breaking down. We talked about all the things I wanted to do to the shed, the practical things, like heat and light and walls without holes in and a roof that didn't leak, and the things I wanted to change for the sake of aesthetics. I wanted to sand the floorboards, take off the years of grime that had accumulated on them. I wanted to make them look like the expensively distressed floorboards in the houses that featured in the magazines my sister read. I was sure I would be much happier inside if I painted one or two of the tongue-and-groove walls with some expensive chalky paint, like Farrow & Ball.

It was no surprise I felt this way. It wasn't just my sister's house that was full of magazines about interior decoration. They were all over the doctor's surgery. The newspapers had special supplements. The message was always the same: if we could get our houses to look and feel right, then we would look and feel right too. Never mind that many of the people who read the magazines probably didn't even have houses to alter and improve, and, if they did have houses, most of them would be struggling enough just to make the mortgage payments. Never mind that tenants had virtually no rights left and therefore probably wouldn't dare to make any home improvements. Never mind that homelessness was a serious and growing problem, along with mental illness, loneliness and poverty. I suspected that houses and homes were central to the culture of aspiration precisely *because* they were unaffordable. We could dream, and the fact that none of us could actually afford to live in this fabricated reality was part of the strategy. The dream kept us going, kept us working, kept us striving.

Consumer debt kept the economy growing. As far as the voracious economy was concerned, it was crucial that nobody was ever satisfied, crucial that the mass of men remained desperate, crucial that nobody felt secure.

According to Robert Sullivan, Thoreau was also surrounded by house-building and home-making literature. He even suggests that *Walden* can be read as a parody of this aspirational culture:

> In his parody, Thoreau is able to address the matter at hand, building a house, while alluding to the larger subject, getting a living, or life, especially at a time when . . . the machinations of the economy are kicking some people out of their houses and into cities or unemployment, while offering other people country houses, a trade-off.[40]

'Having a glass door in the back wall is my biggest dream,' I explained to the boatbuilder as we turned off the A30 and navigated a maze of industrial and housing estates. 'I'd be able to sit inside my shed and watch the sunset.'

'Well, there's no harm in dreaming,' said the boatbuilder, 'but what are you doing for work?'

'Panicking,' I said.

We finally stopped in front of a shop with dozens of woodburners on display in the window. I felt a surge of excitement. The shed was going to be seriously cosy with a woodburner in it. I was going to be warm. If I was skint, I could burn dead gorse from the cliffs. That's what people in the village used to do. It's good for the living gorse to remove the dead matter, and, if gorse is properly dead, it burns really well. It doesn't even need to be seasoned. I knew this first-hand from years of beach fires and impromptu barbecues.

Back at the shed, the boatbuilder made a list of the things that needed to be done to make it upright and watertight, while I arranged my purchases around the old woodburner, which I was slowly cleaning with a wire brush. We couldn't fit the woodburner yet, because the roof needed fixing first and I needed a hearth and I needed to take the tongue and groove off from behind where the stove was going to go and replace it with something fireproof, like heavy-duty plasterboard.

After the boatbuilder left, I drove to my sister's village to check the surf. The waves were not inviting, so I walked along the beach instead. Before I drove back to the shed, I gathered up the rubbish bags I had been storing in my car and put them in the big bin by the beach. Someone I considered to be a friend saw me. I had known him and his wife since long before they were married. I had played records at their wedding.

'Pay council tax and you can get your own bin!' he shouted.

I laughed, but I couldn't tell if he was joking. I had looked into paying council tax, but I was too scared to tell the council I was living in my shed. What to do with our rubbish was one of the problems Charlie and I both experienced. Another one was voting. I was lucky, because my sister said I could register at her house. It was in another village, so it meant I had no say over what happened in my village. But at least it meant I could vote in general elections. Charlie couldn't find anywhere to register. She didn't vote.

On Monday, the boatbuilder called me again.

'Are you still panicking?' he said.

'Yes.'

'We're a man down, over here. Do you fancy a few weeks on a building site?'

'Doing what?'

'Fixing slates, cutting Celotex and plasterboard.'

'I've never done any of that before,' I said.

'Don't worry,' said the boatbuilder. 'The boys will show you what to do.'

There were three of us working full-time on the house: me, the boatbuilder, who everyone called Boss, even though his name was actually Bill, and Mike the mason. Various others came and went. Some of them, like the roofer, stayed for weeks. Others, like the plumber and the electrician, came several times a week, for a few hours each time. Sometimes, there were six of us at lunchtime, sitting on the floor with our sandwiches and cups of tea, or, if it was sunny, up on the roofer's scaffolding, shoulder to shoulder with the seagulls, who guarded their chimney pots like Norman barons in their castles.

I was nervous when I started on the building site. It was like the first day at a new school, where I was the youngest in the year by miles, and the only girl. The builders spoke a special kind of made-up language of banter and jargon, which I didn't understand. I couldn't help wondering if the jokes were at my expense. I tried to make up for my lack of skills by grafting as hard as I could. I made tea and swept the floor and gathered up all the rubbish. I carried things that were too heavy, to prove I was one of the boys. I learned how to use a drill, cut slates, and intuit correctly whether measurements were in centimetres or inches.

The client, who was rumoured to make his living designing military drones for the government, wasn't there very often. I don't know if it was true about the military drones, but I do know that he paid us all with brand-new fifty-pound notes, and told us that we didn't need to declare them for tax, if we didn't want to.

I did want to declare mine for tax. I couldn't afford to pay an accountant, so I did my tax return myself, and I found the tax system terrifying, with all its incomprehensible rules and regulations. Because I didn't know what I could claim for, I hardly claimed for anything. I felt like I was about to be arrested and dragged off to prison every time I logged on to my HMRC account. And then there were tax *credits*. I was encouraged to apply for tax credits when I first registered as self-employed, in my mid-twenties. The amount I received went up and down, depending on my tax return. Some years, it was so small it might as well have been nothing. Other years, it was enough to cover some of my direct debits, like car insurance and national insurance. Tax credits were a buffer against the precarious nature of my freelance lifestyle, helping to mitigate against the worst effects of an income that fluctuated wildly with the seasons. Unfortunately, tax credits weren't designed to underwrite the fluctuating incomes of people on zero hours contracts. They were a form of corporate socialism, designed to prop up the poverty wages (and executive bonuses) paid by old-fashioned employers like Tesco. I'd been investigated twice, and both times I'd nearly had a nervous breakdown. Even though the mountains of proof I provided, the bank statements and invoices and receipts and diaries, were enough to convince them I was not a cheat or a fraudster, I still felt like one, and I wondered if the very modest payments were worth the stress.

The fifty-pound notes were stressful too. They were the old kind, which were being phased out, and, although they were still legal, many shops refused to take them. When I took the notes to the bank, I felt like a criminal. The teller would call her manager and he would look me up on the money-laundering database, then check each note carefully to see if it was fake, while a queue formed behind me.

It was money, though. Added to the two thousand pounds, it meant all sorts of things for the shed. The first thing it meant was electricity. The electrician on the building site gave me the number of someone who would check the wiring and the plug sockets, without sucking his teeth and muttering dark threats about calling the council. Once this was done, I arranged for EDF to send an engineer to install a new meter. I paid the outstanding bill and a year upfront. The whole thing cost a thousand pounds, but it was worth it. I thought it was worth it, anyway, until I actually turned the lights on.

The change was devastating. The light from the bare bulbs that were fixed to the ends of wires that hung down from the ceiling was cold and harsh. The shed looked like a shed again, not a home. It looked dirty and sad. I tried plugging one of my turntables in, the one that still had a phono lead attached to it, but it didn't work.

There was nothing to be done. I had paid for the electricity to be turned on. Electricity was progress and there was no going back from it. The word 'progress' is from the Latin pro which means forward, and *gradi*, which means advance. It was like the tide that carried us around Land's End when we paddled from the west-facing beach on our surfboards. I'd paid for a year upfront. That was that. I reminded myself of all the things I could do now, that I hadn't been able to do before. I could plug in my laptop and type words on to a screen, instead of scrawling them in the half-dark with a pencil. I could read all night without straining my eyes. I could listen to records – once I'd fixed my turntables. Electricity was a good thing, I reminded myself, every time I got the sick feeling of loss in the pit of my stomach, and soon enough I believed it and I forgot what life had been like before.

Brute Neighbours

A man is rich in proportion to the number
of things which he can afford to let alone.

I threw myself into fixing and improving the shed, and it was certainly true that electricity made this easier. I bought a Hoover. The boatbuilder came across some big sheets of corrugated iron, going spare, or so he said. He cut them to size with an angle grinder and I spent a whole weekend on the roof, riding my shed through the sky, like it was a horse, disturbing the crows, who flapped away in a rage whenever I pressed the trigger on the drill. The boatbuilder handed me the sheets of corrugated iron and I fixed them. It was hard work. I insisted on putting the new sheets on top of the old sheets, because I didn't want to disturb the sparrows' nest. The shed was their home, too. I had to line up the sheets and somehow hold them in place – no mean feat on a late October day, with a fresh northerly wind and occasional hail storms – long enough to drill through the two layers of metal and then hammer a huge flat-headed nail through the hole and into the shed itself, which shuddered and seemed about to collapse.

I was so engrossed with transforming the shed, I forgot I was meant to be pretending I didn't live there. Everyone could see me up there on the roof. Mostly, I ignored the cars that slowed to a crawl to get a better look at what I was doing. I had other things on my mind. When the roof was done, the boatbuilder would plug in his grinder and cut a hole for the chimney pipe, which was still leaning up against the tongue and groove. We had salvaged a broken slate from the client's house, which was going to be my hearth, and some bricks for it to stand on. We had already taken off the tongue and groove behind the hearth and replaced it with heat-resistant plasterboard. October was nearly over. Soon, the clocks would go back. The shed was cold and damp. I couldn't wait to light my first fire.

On the days I worked on the building site, I went to the boat-builder's cottage afterwards for a shower. We spent so much time together, it felt like we were living together. Sometimes, I would stand in the front room of his cottage, warming my hands by his fire, and I would think about the shed and I would wonder if it wasn't time to leave, to let it go, to rejoin the rest of civilization. There was a spare room in the boatbuilder's cottage. There was hot water and a fridge and lots of different rooms. I would be cared for. I knew that. There was space for me in the boatbuilder's life, and part of me longed to lean backwards into it. But his life wasn't my life, and I had made that mistake before.

The boatbuilder – he never seemed like Boss to me, and even less like Bill – gave up all his weekends to help me. He still refused to take my money, so I stored the help away in my mind, hoping that one day I would find a way to repay him. In the meantime, my money went on materials. I scoured the county for second-hand windows and doors. I bought batons and posts to rebuild the parts of the shed that were damaged beyond repair. I was given a single bed, which another friend had made for his daughter, who had since grown up, and I installed it where the board bag used to be, under the back window. I ordered a foam mattress from IKEA. When it wasn't being a bed, the bed was a sofa.

Chris found an old glass door in a partly rotten frame and gave it to me, and the boatbuilder made a new frame for it from offcuts lying around in his workshop. One evening, he cut a hole in the west-facing wall and hung it for me. The shed was transformed – full of light, where before it had been dark. I didn't have to go by the road every time I wanted water, or a wee, or a shower. I could lie on the floorboards in a patch of sunlight and read or watch the sky, until it got dark.

I had often heard people with houses talk about how much work it was doing them up and maintaining them and renovating them and turning them into homes. They were right. It was hard and it was messy and even the smallest task seemed to take forever. Every time I solved a problem, I made at least one new one. The light from the new door meant I urgently had to do something about the state of the old floorboards, which were black with dirt and grime. I borrowed the boatbuilder's electric sander and sanded them. It took me four days, crawling around on my hands and knees, wearing a mask and goggles, cursing. By the time I had finished sanding, all my possessions were covered with a thick layer of dust. I sat back on my knees and surveyed my kingdom. Homes aren't just about aspiration, they're about nest-building. Living in rented accommodation, on short-term tenancies, where there is no opportunity to invest time and effort in homemaking, means missing out on one of life's great pleasures. It was hard work, but the satisfaction of creating a home for myself made up for the work a hundred times over.

Finally, it was time to light the woodburner. Everything was ready. The baffle board had been hammered into place. I had scrubbed at the rust until my fingers were raw. The chimney was attached and secured, inside and out. The heat-resistant silicone had been expertly applied. The fire cement was drying. I gathered an armful of dried gorse from the cliffs and bought a basket to store it in. I collected ten plastic sacks' worth of offcuts and kindling from the building site. I lined them up against the south-facing end of the shed and covered them with the bit of tarpaulin that used to be over the hole. I sat in the cold shed and waited.

It was the fifth of November. My sister was present for the ceremony, and so was the boatbuilder. I gathered up my jam jars and poured us all a finger of whisky from the bottle I had bought the boatbuilder to say thank you. Fireworks were going off all over the village, their energy exploding and turning into fleeting galaxies of stars that dissolved and disappeared. We drank the whisky standing on the pallets, watching the fire-works, until it got too cold and we went inside.

The boatbuilder checked the baffle board one last time, then he handed me a box of matches. I was suddenly terri-fied. What if the fire cement and the heat-resistant silicone didn't work? What if the shed went up in flames, and all my possessions with it? I remembered the time I'd burned Dad's papers, the height and ferocity of the flames. My hand shook as I struck the match and held it against the paper. The paper took. I closed the door with its new glass and secured it with the catch the boatbuilder's friend had made in his metalworks. The shed creaked and groaned as the moisture was pushed out of its old timbers.

'Do it the world of good,' said the boatbuilder.

Later, when I was alone, I stretched out in front of the fire like a cat, enjoying the warmth from the floorboards soaking into my bones. I went outside and watched the smoke curling out of the chimney – my chimney – then I went back inside and put more wood on the fire – my fire. I sat cross-legged in front of it, staring at the flames. I felt the heat burning the tension out of my body. The fire was still burning when I went to bed. I lay in bed, watching the flames from my own hearth flicker in the darkness.

But there is no fire without smoke, and a plume of smoke rising from a chimney says *home* like nothing else does. I had crossed an invisible line, had forgotten that even though it felt like home, more and more with every passing day, the shed was not a home. Even though I dwelt there, harming nobody, as far as I could tell, the shed was not a dwelling, and dwelling in it was not allowed.

The letter arrived on Tuesday. It was in a brown envelope stamped with the Cornwall Council motto: *All for One and One for All*. I read the letter, and then I crumpled it up into a ball and lay, face down, on the floor.

Dear Sir/Madam,

RE: ALLEGED UNAUTHORIZED RESIDENTIAL OCCUPATION OF SHED: JUNCTION OF MAIN ROAD (CROSSROADS).

I refer to the above matter, which has recently been brought to the attention of this department.

To enable the Planning Investigation Team to investigate this matter, I would be grateful if you would contact me to discuss the situation and arrange a mutually convenient date and time for a meeting at the above property.

Please endeavour to do so within 14 days from the date of this letter.

Yours faithfully,

Planning Enforcement Officer.

Winter Visitors

We talked of rude and simple times, when
men sat about large fires in cold, bracing weather,
with clear heads.

It was three in the morning and my head was all over the place. My thoughts were circling the letter, viewing it from different angles, trying to decide what it meant.

It was cold. The old woodburner was so warped it didn't seal properly and wouldn't shut down. It was either lit, and burning furiously, or out. I was careful about lighting it because of the effort of finding and chopping wood. At three in the morning, the uninsulated shed was roughly the same temperature as outdoors: about four degrees. I got up to make a fresh hot-water bottle. There was no water in the kettle. I opened my new back door and fumbled for the tap in the dark. There were stars, but I didn't notice them.

I wrapped a blanket Mum had given me around my shoulders and leaned on the cupboard that was my kitchen, waiting for the water to boil. The rats and mice were visiting again, now that the temperature had plummeted, looking for food and warmth. I could hear them scrabbling away in the wall cavities.

It was only a matter of time before they ate their way in and started doing victory laps of the shed, keeping me awake all night and falling asleep in my muesli. I couldn't poison them anymore, because of what I knew about barn owls. I couldn't live with them running around the shed every night either. I didn't know what I was going to do.

I didn't know what I was going to do about the council either. If only the letter had come earlier. Up until a few weeks ago, the shed still looked like a broken shed. It would have been hard to believe anyone was actually living in it. But now, with the new door and the chimney, the clothes rail, the bed, the freshly sanded floorboards, it looked like a home. I would have to eradicate myself again. My heart sank. I would have to shove all my possessions in the car, dismantle the bed, or disguise it somehow, make it look like a sofa. I would have to take my pictures off the walls and take the clothes rail apart. But there was nothing I could do about the woodburner.

I had contacted the planning office on the number at the top of the letter and made an appointment for them to visit me in three weeks' time. Their idea, not mine. I didn't have a choice. The person I spoke to wasn't the enforcement officer, and she let slip during the course of the conversation that the reason for the letter was that somebody had complained. I wanted to know who it was, but she said it was confidential. It had to be the woodburner, the smoky evidence that I was settling in, getting comfortable, planning to stay.

I went over to my desk and crouched down and pulled out

my massive dictionary. I found the box with the magnifying glass, then I flicked through the dictionary until I got to *D*. I traced the tiny letters with my finger until I found what I was looking for. There it was. The Old Danish *dvale*, which meant trance or stupor. Finally, I understood. The trance of staring into the flames of a real fire, the stupor of relaxation that went with being at home, from the Indo-European root *dheu*, meaning dust, cloud, vapour or smoke. The contrails of a dwelling, the proof of a hearth and therefore a home.

The kettle boiled. My thoughts were circling the letter again. Was I going to be evicted? How would that happen in practice? What would the council do if they tried to evict me and I refused to leave? If I lied and said I wasn't living there, which was what my sister was advocating (*I don't know why you're so worried, what are they actually going to do?*), would they send officers round in the middle of the night? Would they install cameras? Would the person who complained keep complaining?

Would they knock the shed down, like they had knocked down the poet's hut? No, the shed wasn't the problem. I was the problem. The shed was allowed to be there, it was me that wasn't. It was about change of use, the person on the phone had said, breezily. It felt like life and death.

I poured the boiling water into the hot-water bottle and put it in the bed, then I went back to the dictionary. I turned to *F*. 'Freedom' was from the Old English *freodom*, which meant power of self-determination, state of free will, emancipation from slavery, deliverance.

I put the dictionary away and climbed into bed. I was reading *A Room of One's Own*, but it wasn't helping. I didn't need to be reminded that literature was strewn with the wreckage of those who had 'minded beyond reason the opinion of others' or that 'a woman must have money and a room of her own if she is to write fiction'. The corners of the shed were full of the shadows of spiders that didn't exist. Huge, black spiders, with eyes on stalks, that crouched and waited, biding their time, ready to run full-tilt at me when I least expected it, or climb in my mouth while I was sleeping. The thought of it made the hairs on my body stand on end.

I got up again and went back to the desk and found *Anxiety*. The dictionary explained that, in the 1520s, 'anxiety' meant 'apprehension caused by danger, misfortune, or error, uneasiness of mind respecting some uncertainty, a restless dread of some evil.'

What the dictionary didn't explain was how it felt to be anxious. How it felt to feel so scared that even breathing was difficult, never mind sleeping. To live with a constant terror that made even the simplest things impossible: making phone calls, posting letters. It wasn't there all the time, thankfully, but it had been there on and off since I was ten and had first confronted concepts like death and infinity. That was when I'd realized that even my parents, *especially* my parents, were vulnerable and insecure and had no idea what was going on.

My parents headed south from their native Wales for the best of reasons. They wanted to give us a magical childhood that was made of more than economics, and they succeeded. But economics caught up with them in the end. My childhood ended on Black Wednesday, when Britain crashed out of the Exchange Rate Mechanism and interest rates doubled overnight. Dad's business went under. My parents could no longer afford to pay the mortgage. The solid structures of family and home quickly disintegrated. There was nothing to hold on to except unfolding uncertainty, the looming threat of homelessness, free school meals eaten in the canteen while my friends bought pasties in town, guilt and confusion about the money my grandad left me and summer jobs at Land's End that paid three pounds fifty an hour.

Not knowing who had complained was the worst part. I had begun to feel like I belonged in the village and now I suspected everyone of wanting to get rid of me. I was suspicious of my neighbours when they smiled at me. Were they secretly plotting to have me removed? Why? Was it the fishermen who had the allotments? But they left me vegetables and waited by the gate out of politeness when they happened to arrive to tend their gardens just as I was enjoying a naked hose-down in the shower tray. That must surely count for something. I tried to put my mind to the practical question of what I would actually do if I had to leave. Where I would go. What I would do with those castles in the air that had been slowly taking on real foundations for the past six months.

There was no more work with the boatbuilder. The team had disbanded. Everyone except me had moved to different jobs. I had saved enough fifty-pound notes to last a few months, if I was careful and didn't buy anything except food, and if I didn't suddenly have to spend it on rent and a deposit. I had been feeling positive about the winter. I was going to start writing the book I'd been talking about for so long it was getting embarrassing. I had it all worked out. If I ran out of money I would busk carols in Truro in the run-up to Christmas. The shed was warm(ish) and watertight. I had a desk and electricity. This was it. This was my chance.

Only now all I could think about was the council. I distracted myself by thinking about rats. I drove to the scrap-metal yard and asked a man with no front teeth if he had any rolls or strips of metal. The idea had come to me one sleepless night, when I was searching for ways to occupy my mind. I pictured a thin layer of metal attached to the base of the wooden walls, all the way around the shed, like a skirting board. They wouldn't be able to chew their way through *metal*, would they? The man with no front teeth guffawed, and told me that rats could chew their way through titanium. He told me to buy a roll of tiling mesh from the builders' merchant. 'Wear gloves,' he said. Tiling mesh was sharp as razors and would cut my hands to bits.

It was easy to understand why people used rat poison. I spent a whole day crawling around the spidery edges of the shed with a hammer and nails and this awful razor-sharp mesh. I rolled it out slowly, making a little lip which I hammered into the floor and hammering the other edge into the uprights or, where there were no uprights (which was most of the time), directly into the tongue and groove. Cutting it was the worst part. I had to cut each little razor bit separately, with wire cutters. By the time I'd finished, I had deep cuts all over my wrists and fingers, in spite of the gloves. The tongue and groove cracked and splintered when I hammered it, because there was nothing behind it apart from air. The shed shuddered and shook. I pictured the boatbuilder's horrified face. I pressed on. The tiling mesh made the shed look like a penal institution. It looked so bad, I went back to the builders' merchant and bought lengths of timber to fix over the top of it. That was easier said than done. I discovered undulations in the floor of the shed. Time had caused the floorboards to sink between the floor joists. Also, the walls weren't vertical. When I finished fixing my rat-proof skirting board, there were big gaps between the wood and the floor and the wood and the walls. The gaps needed filling, not just for aesthetic reasons, but because of the spiders that would no doubt take the gaps for a home. I went back to the builders' merchant for silicone and tiny batons. At least I knew what these things were called, now that I had worked as a builder. Perhaps it was my destiny to *be* a builder. It was a shame I was so crap at it.

All of this took the best part of a week. I was just finishing when there was a knock at the door. I flinched. I wasn't expecting the council for another week. Or had I got the day wrong? Was it *this* week? They wouldn't come in the evening, though. Shit, shit, shit. I stood up and transferred some of the

silicone that was all over my hands on to my jeans. I opened
the door. It was my old best friend from the valley.

'Mum said you were living here!' she said. 'Such *fun*.'

I stared at her. Twenty years had passed since we made dens
and beelines and spun each other round on the capstan in the
cove, but my friend – my oldest friend in the whole wide world
– looked and sounded exactly the same.

I lit the fire and we sat on the floor in front of it, drinking a
bottle of wine I had opened the night before. My friend told me
about her husband's work as a barrister and her three children
and how she lived in London in the house we all stayed in the
time her mum took us to Hamleys and the Science Museum.
Did I remember? Of course I did. It was my first experience of
being in a big city, or any city. I remembered the lights and the
noise and the hustle, the black cabs and red buses and burnt-
clutch smell of the Underground. London. Exciting, horrifying
London. How could I forget?

When it came to telling her about my life, I couldn't think
what to say. I had no children, no husband, no job. I was proud
of the way the shed was looking, but I didn't want to talk about
it, because of the looming council visit. I was a hermit crab and
the shed was my shell. I felt naked at the thought of losing it,
undefended and powerless.

I put another piece of gorse in the woodburner. My friend
told me about the house she and her husband had bought at
the top of the valley, which was where she was staying, how
they'd had the builders in and the builders had made a mess

and it was chaos and now they were painting. I listened to her cheerful banter and tried to work out when it was that I'd lost that easy confidence. I had it once. I could almost remember how it felt. It was similar to how I felt after surfing waves I was scared of, or at least paddling out in them and not drowning.

'Do you remember when we climbed up that massive cliff?' I said, suddenly. 'All the way to the top. We were crazy. We could have died!'

'It was your idea,' said my friend. 'Do you remember how we used to dare each other to swim out to the buoy? You used to go blue, you got so cold.'

'Do you remember selling those bits of asbestos we found in the river?'

We were both laughing now.

'We tried to sell my sister.'

'We left her in the hedge and told her we were playing that she'd been kidnapped. We left her there for hours.'

'Do you remember when I bit you in school because you ruined the picture we had made?'

'Do you remember when you cut your foot in our pond and had to go to hospital?'

Do you remember, do you remember, do you remember . . . ?

I remembered that confidence had its roots in trust, and that I used to trust the world and I used to trust *myself*, but somewhere along the way I had decided the world could not be trusted, and I could not be trusted to make my way in it. There was a hollow place inside me where that confidence used to be.

After my friend left, I lay on the bed, watching the stars through the window. Sometimes, the stars looked like the twinkling lights of a hundred million households, an inter-galactic village that included me and my shed within its boundaries, a necessary dot in the vast and intricate pattern of the universe. That night, the stars were just leftover energy, burning itself out in the void.

I felt an emptiness opening up inside of me. I wondered what it would take for me to feel safe, for the fear to go away. Money could buy security – but it was only an illusion, because money could be lost. Before the letter came, I'd felt safe in my shed, but that was an illusion too. I was a soft-skinned creature, living in a cold climate, who could not produce her own food. Without the shed, I would be skinless again, crashing through space with nothing to break my fall, subject to the whims of markets and other people. I felt a rush of vertigo and thought about what happened to my parents, especially Mum. I knew she loved me fiercely, and I loved her fiercely in return, but knowing is not the same as feeling, and depression can feel like rejection. Mum's illness took her far away from us. She was stuck on the wrong side of an invisible wall, and I couldn't bring her back. The years of upheaval that followed my enchanted early childhood were defined by loss. Mum, Dad, the house we lived in, the story I told myself about who I was and how I fitted in.

I thought about my friend, how we had started off equal, then grown less and less equal over the years. It had something to do with claims to fame and ancestry, being able to trace your path backwards through bricks and institutions. My friend's path was well marked. It had not, as far as I could tell, surprised or disappointed her. She did not appear to have surprised or disappointed herself. Her story was intact. The structures her childhood had been built on were still standing. It struck me that man-made systems and structures, like property, class and money, were a kind of insulation against the reality of fate and chance and change. The power and control they represented allowed trust to flourish and confidence to grow. The opposite was a vicious cycle of dispossession, which stripped away self-esteem until the smallest risks seemed too terrible to contemplate. My friend and I had both unconsciously internalized a narrative that said people's gifts and capabilities could be measured in terms of property, and we trusted ourselves accordingly. But the kind of confidence that has its roots in property is compromised, because property is an illusion. Reality is made of change, destruction and decay.

My story would have been very different, I'm sure, if I'd grown up somewhere else. I was lucky enough to be able to take refuge in the outdoors, and I found comfort and security in nature.

Ever since I could walk, I was allowed to run wild. I explored as far as my legs could carry me. I was shy and anxious and struggled to feel confident around people, but, by the time I was twelve, I knew every inch of the peninsula. I had seen the sun rise out of the sea countless times, getting up at the crack of dawn and sliding out of the house before anyone woke up. I had followed every river back to its source and worked out where to swim when the sea was rough and the wind was blowing a gale. I knew secret hollows in the cliffs where nobody would ever find me, and I made myself at home in them, using them to cry in peace.

The easy confidence my friend possessed appeared to be founded on the man-made structures that had randomly persisted, so far, for her. But maybe there was another kind of confidence, one that is founded on the laws of nature; the knowledge that everything is temporary, even stone.

I didn't eradicate myself. The only thing I did was borrow cushions and a throw from Charlie, to make the bed look more like a sofa. I tried to research planning policy and find precedents online, but even typing the words *planning enforcement officer* into Google made me feel sick with anxiety. The only thing I found that was vaguely reassuring was a thread where someone had written that, if they wanted to evict me, they had to prove I was causing harm. I wondered if a garden that smelled of wee counted as harm.

The morning of the visit, I was up at dawn. I sat on the concrete doorstep, wrapped in blankets, waiting for the sun to come stealing up the road and find my face. Eventually, a black Ford Focus slowed down and stopped on the other side of the crossroads. Someone got out and walked towards me.

'What happened here?' said the planning enforcement officer, frowning at the twisted chevrons, as if it was me who'd mangled them.

'I was crashed into,' I said. 'They were driving too fast and missed the corner.'

The planning enforcement officer wrote something on her clipboard. The planning enforcement officer was a woman. This was the first surprise. The second was that I liked her. Or, if I didn't exactly like her, I didn't hate her either. I felt that she was on my side, or at least she wasn't exactly against me. She was close to my age, for one thing. I hadn't realized I was old enough to be the same age as a planning enforcement officer.

'We were told somebody was living here,' said the planning enforcement officer, once we were inside.

I swallowed, but said nothing.

'Who owns the building?'

'My dad.'

'And who uses it?'

'Me.'

'Does your dad know you use it?'

'Yes.'

'What do you use it for?'

'Writing.'

I gestured towards the laptop, which I had turned on and placed in the centre of the desk, along with a random selection of notebooks and the massive dictionary. I had left the magnifying glass over the word *entitled*. Just in case.

'How long have you been using it for?'

'I started using it in March.'

The planning enforcement officer wrote something on her clipboard.

'It's very cold,' she said.

'Yes.'

'Does this work?'

She pointed at the wood-burning stove.

'Yes,' I said, 'but I don't use it in the day. I mean, I only use it on the *coldest* days.'

The planning enforcement officer walked around the shed. She stopped to look at each of my photographs, especially the one of my yellow van parked by a fjord, with mountains in the distance and my cello, on its side, on the rocky ground. She looked at me and narrowed her eyes, and, for some reason, I had a clear image of the man with the bare feet and crazed expression and matted hair who lived, for a time, in a cave just the other side of Land's End. He'd come into the cafe where I worked as a teenager, and sit in the corner and eat a bowl of soup, which the owners of the cafe gave him for free, because he had no money. Then one day he didn't come, and nobody ever saw him again.

Her gaze fell on the bed, which was not-so-cunningly disguised as a sofa. She turned to me.

'Where do you live, Miss Davies?'

It was then that I realised she didn't care. This was just another game that had to be played. Boxes had to be ticked. The machine had to be appeased.

I gave the name of my sister's village and the planning enforcement officer wrote it down on her clipboard.

'I'll need you to write a letter,' she said, 'confirming that you don't live here and including your home address.'

I took a deep breath. If this was a game, then they could at least tell me the rules.

'What if I *was* living here?' I said.

'You would be breaking the law.'

'Why?'

'Because the law says that this is not a dwelling.'

'What would make it a dwelling?'

'Planning permission. But you wouldn't get it.'

'Why not?'

'We don't give consent for new dwellings where there are no amenities, and there has to be development on three sides.'

'But it isn't new. This building has been here for seventy years.'

'That's not relevant.'

'Why not?'

'It just isn't.'

'What *kind* of amenities?'

'There would need to be a pavement to the shops.'

I felt hysteria building up inside me. I mustn't laugh. I must not laugh. I took deep breaths.

'What happens if someone else complains?'

'We visit you again.'

'You just keep on visiting?'

'At least once every three years.'

Winter Animals

It is remarkable how many creatures live wild
and free though secret in the woods.

It was because of the four-year rule, my sister said. In her research, which was far more extensive than mine, she had found out that, if you lived somewhere you weren't supposed to for four years, and could prove it, and didn't get any complaints in that time, then you could apply for a certificate of lawfulness. It was not a given that the application would be approved. If the person granting the certificate decided you had tried to hide what you were doing, for instance, they could refuse it. Or if the evidence was not compelling.

'What sort of evidence?'

My sister and I were sitting in her kitchen, drinking strong black coffee made in a cafetière. She read from a list on the screen of the laptop that was open in front of her.

'Letters, especially official ones, like bank statements. Utility bills. Photographs. Signed affidavits from professional people, like doctors and lawyers. Receipts for furniture, like beds and mattresses, showing the date it was moved in.'

'I've got to write a letter giving my home address, and it can't be there.'

'Hmm, that's not ideal.' My sister got up to let her dog in, who was whining at the door that led into her garden. 'You can use this address, but then they'll have it on file that you said you didn't live there, and that might count as hiding. Not much you can do about that, though. If I were you, I'd write the letter and, at the same time, I'd change everything so it gets sent to the shed instead of here. Bank, tax, all that stuff. Change your driving licence.'

'I feel like a criminal,' I said.

'Don't be stupid,' said my sister, sitting back down and pouring herself more coffee. 'You're just being strategic. It's a game, remember.'

I left my sister's house and walked along the beach, which was completely deserted, following the tideline. It was nearly the end of November and there was a storm coming. I could see it in the colour of the sky. The sea was too wild for surfing. The beach was completely empty of humans. I thought about the seals swimming out to the safety of deep water with their pups. Sometimes the pups got lost and washed up on the beaches. When people tried to help them, they lashed out with their teeth and tails.

I got wet feet crossing the stream. On the other side of the stream, in the dunes, I saw the blackened stones of old fires, like the ghosts of summer. It was only a few months since August, but I couldn't even imagine summer. Summer was an alien concept. I turned to walk back to my car. The sky had darkened so much, it was hard to tell where exactly it met the sea. The hail, when it came, was violent, like handfuls of stones being hurled in my face. I started to run. I wanted to get home, light the fire, thaw out the shed. I felt like I had been running hurdles for months, jumping through one hoop after another, being tested again and again. I was glad it was winter, glad it was hailing. I wanted to close the door and shut everything out for a while.

The world seemed to turn more slowly as the shortest day approached. The nights were so long that, some days, surfing was impossible, even if the waves were okay, because there wasn't enough day each side of high tide. Chris gave me a skateboard, a long one that even I could ride. I used it for collecting firewood from the empty cliffs. I rode it to the end of the long straight tarmac lane, then stashed it in the hedge near the farmhouse. I collected dried gorse into a bundle and wrapped it in a coat, then rode the skateboard back again, with the bundle of gorse on my head.

Storms went on for days, then weeks. I learned to sleep like a baby through them, even when the shed clanged and shook and rattled like a wooden boat being washed on to rocks. There were days when the peninsula was wrapped in a cloud so dense you couldn't see the sea until you were standing in it, and, if you took your chances and paddled out, within seconds, you couldn't see the shore.

I bought a thermometer and kept it on the shelf by my bed.

Some mornings, it showed four degrees. Some mornings, it showed two. I learned to fill the kettle before I went to sleep, because some mornings the outside tap was frozen. I fell into the habit of running over the cliffs to the cove in the mornings, wearing Jan Erik's jumper. Being hot and sweaty helped with washing under the outside tap.

Most of the birds had fled to easier climates. The corvids were strutting around like they owned the place, bolshy rooks and crows and magpies. Ravens lurked among the boulders, casting spells with their beady eyes. The gannets and gulls spent all their time fishing, and so did the seals, diving deep under the breakers to avoid being smashed to pieces against the cliffs. I tried to imagine being one of those seals, and failed. According to a Werner Herzog documentary called *Encounters at the End of the World*, seals hear through their whiskers and the sounds they make resemble a kind of futuristic synthesizer: loud pops and squiggles and bleeps.

My life was physically demanding. I depended on my body. I'd always put so much energy into working out exactly what was wrong with my body, exactly how it didn't conform to the images of perfection I had in my head, that I'd never even noticed how strong it was. Trying to achieve an unnaturally skinny body had left me weak – not just physically but psychologically. Divided from myself, I was easier to rule. Now, my imperfections started to look like strengths. A healthy appetite allowed me to convert porridge into the energy I needed to run for miles, gathering firewood, an exercise for which my sturdy legs were perfect. My arms were strong enough to lug big bundles of it back to the shed, along with huge pieces of driftwood to make furniture. Everyone I knew got winter colds and flu, but I stayed stubbornly healthy. My sister said it was breathing all the fresh air that blew in through the holes in the walls and the floor of the shed, and that some people paid good money to immerse themselves in cold water, because it boosted the immune system. I thought about our ancestors on their hill farms in Wales, collecting water and gathering firewood and feeding and killing their animals, wading through mud that came up to their knees. I don't suppose they ever longed for slender, delicate legs. They were gifted the legs they needed, and they passed them on to me.

The shortest day came and went, then Christmas, then New Year. The rats and mice gave it everything they had, but they couldn't break through the tiling mesh. My muesli was safe. I was snug and cosy.

I ordered books on writing from Amazon and read them sitting cross-legged in front of the woodburner. It was hot in my shed when the fire was going, hotter than my sister's house, which had a wood-fired Rayburn, unless the wind was blowing from the west, in which case the fire wouldn't light at all. The wind pushed air down the chimney, the shed filled up with smoke, and the crossroads filled up with the sound of me cursing. The geese and the ducks who lived on the pond travelled further and further to find food. Sometimes, I'd come home to find them rummaging for worms in the space where

I parked my car. They shouted and hissed and flapped at me when I tried to move them on.

It rained and rained and the surface of the earth melted into mud. When the rain stopped, there were starlings, vast mushroom clouds of birds, flying themselves like a kite over the barren fields. Farmers covered the fields in plastic, making it look like it had snowed. I gathered seaweed from the beach and from the cove at the bottom of the slipway, where Justin and I had drunk our flat whites in the summer sun. I spread it on my vegetable beds and covered them with old bits of carpet and plywood I found in skips.

I didn't travel very far, because I didn't have money for diesel, but I had plenty of books, and what I lost in range, I gained in depth. I saw things that winter I'd never seen before, even though I had lived on the peninsula for most of my life. The world seemed to get smaller and bigger at the same time. On the one hand, there was the mundane repetition of the things I had to do to survive, and, on the other hand, there was the vast ocean and the empty cliffs and the great tent of a sky that filled up with stars on clear nights. The fact that the stars existed many hundreds of millions of light years away put the usual strain on my imagination. I struggled to hold both realities in my head at the same time: the reality of my daily life, and the reality of the vast and unknowable universe that was the backdrop to it. I stopped worrying about the reason for my existence. The longer I lived in such close proximity to the mysterious earth and the restless ocean and the storms that tore across the peninsula at night and tried to blow my house down, the more I felt that existence itself was significant, and the more I wanted to suck all the marrow out of it, as Thoreau wrote in *Walden*, and not, when I came to die, feel that I hadn't lived.

I loved the sight of the cliffs when they were drenched in rain or mist, looming dormant under the wide sky, guarding the frontier between land and sea. I loved them most when the winds were blowing gales and the air was like a solid wall that could hold me up if I leaned against it. I liked watching the crows ride the currents, fast, out of control, like they were surfing the air. I liked watching them tack back again, facing the extremes of nature, like robust, black-winged sailing boats. The cliffs belonged to the crows in January, and the rabbits and foxes and gulls. It was rumoured that there was a herd of deer living in the stands of pine and sycamore that struggled in their hollows, bent sideways by the wind. I didn't believe the rumours, until the morning I saw a stag.

The stag was standing very still in a patch of bracken, upwind from me. He was so well camouflaged, I almost didn't see him. But there he was, both mythical and real, his head held up high on his delicate neck, his antlers strong and graceful. His nostrils flaring. I tried to slow my breathing down. It was a late January dawn. The sun was rising slowly in the east. I had stopped to watch the clifftops in front of me catch the sunlight bit by bit, as if a wildfire was slowly spreading through the gorse. The stag moved his head from side to side, trying to get a scent. He tiptoed forward, graceful as a ballet dancer, and stopped. Then a wood pigeon saw me and flapped out of the bracken, and then the stag saw me and ran. He ran like he was flying, cleared the hedge between the cliffs and the fields without even breaking his stride, then stopped, turned and waited.

I have no idea why he waited. Perhaps he didn't see me labouring up to the gate and opening it and walking through. He was downwind from me now, so if he couldn't see me, he must at least have smelled me, but he didn't seem to be afraid. He waited on his tiptoes, wearing his magnificent antlers, until I was close enough to see the whites of his eyes and hear the sound of his breathing, and then he was running again. I followed as fast as I could, which was very slowly, compared to him. Once again, he waited. It was like a game, and he knew he was winning. He ran and stopped and waited until I had trespassed almost all the way back to the shed. Then his brown body was streaking through the dead grasses of what used to be the poet's field and he blended into the wet woodland at the far end, and I never saw him again.

The Pond in Winter

I am thankful that this pond was made deep
and pure for a symbol.

All over the peninsula, people were ringing each other up.

'Have you seen it?' they said. 'Have you *seen* it?'

It was out of control. Smashing up the outdoor swimming pool. Throwing rocks at the cars parked on the prom. Taking down the harbour walls. Parking huge boulders in the car parks. Grinding Melissa's lawn into paste. Erasing whole sections of the coast path. Scraping the sand off the beaches. Causing millions of pounds' worth of damage.

Charlie and I watched it from the wall in front of the car park opposite the lord's castle.

'Did you see *that*?' Charlie said. 'Oh my *God*.'

'Do you think they survived?'

'No.'

The swans had looked the way I felt when I was trapped on the inside – the bit near the beach, where the waves are breaking and there's nowhere to hide – and a huge set was coming. They were paddling furiously, trying not to look at the mountains of water rolling towards them. They were further out than usual, on account of the heavy sea, but they hadn't gone far enough. The set caught them, one by one, turned them upside down, spun them around, twisted their delicate necks. I had to cover my eyes with both my hands. Getting caught by a big set and thrown around and held underwater wasn't something I had ever imagined happening to a swan. But these were extraordinary times.

We were at the beach where I used to swim to wash the mud off after a long day in Melissa's garden. It was a very sheltered beach, at the back of the sweeping bay, but that day the waves were too big for surfing. This was such a rare thing that dozens of people were sitting on the wall alongside us, taking pictures on their phones, listening to the sound of billions of fist-sized pebbles being picked up and shaken and put down again. A handful of the most macho men were trying to paddle out. We'd seen them getting changed in the car park. I had my wetsuit and board in Charlie's van, but I was sincerely hoping I wasn't going to have to use them. So far, thank God, even Charlie seemed to think the waves were too big. The macho men weren't getting anywhere. They were getting nailed, like the swans, pushed over and pummelled by the shore break. The human ego is no match for the equalizing effect of the ocean.

It was one of those long-range south-coast swells that had long ago parted ways with the hurricane that created it. The sun was out and there was practically no wind. If I closed my eyes, I could almost imagine it was spring. Apart from the noise.

There was no getting away from the noise. It was everywhere. The booming of air being forced into tiny crevasses in the rock face, the pistol-shot sound of the cliffs cracking under the pressure. The sound of boulders being knocked together. The sound of water on water, tons of it, a frenzy of particles smashing and swirling, caves opening, cliffs falling, waves as high as the headlands, fields covered in foam.

'Have you *seen* it?' Charlie had said, when I called her from the pallets.

'No, but I can hear it.'

I could hear waves breaking on the south-facing beaches, even though they were several miles away.

We drove around the peninsula in Charlie's little red van, supposedly looking for somewhere to surf, in fact just looking at surf. I liked watching people who were braver than me paddle into awful swirling maelstroms. I liked sitting on land and watching people braver than me try to take them on, risking life and limb, not to mention dignity. I could have done that all day, and then gone for a pint. But I knew that, sooner or later, Charlie would want to get in, and that meant I would have to get in, because otherwise I would hate myself forever.

We drove from cove to cove, watching waves break in places where waves never break. I was excited by how disorientated I felt. I might have been in a different country. The peninsula I knew so well seemed barely recognizable. Eventually, we found ourselves in the car park by the beach where we normally surfed. The beach faced north-west, so it was only catching the part of the swell that still had the energy to wrap around Land's End, the ripped-up inconsistent dregs of it, the tip of the tail of the monster. It looked okay from the car park. There was plenty of white water, and the waves looked lumpy and misshapen, but not terrifying. We decided to get in.

'The thing about surfing,' said Charlie, as we carried our boards through the car park, 'is that, sooner or later, you're going to get nailed. The only way you can avoid getting nailed is if you don't get in.'

'Just like life,' I said, 'except, with surfing, you can decide not to get in.'

We had reached the place where the little concrete path that led from the cafe to the sea used to be. The concrete path was missing. I tried to lighten the mood.

'Did you know that bones and shells are stronger than concrete?'

Charlie wasn't listening. 'Crikey,' she said. 'Look, the sand is missing too.'

We clambered over the rocks, where the beach used to be, and looked at the ocean. It was not inviting. It was the exact opposite of inviting. It looked cold, mean, indifferent, grey and deadly. Charlie was staring at the horizon. I knew what she was thinking. We had already put our wetsuits on. That meant we had to get in. It was an unwritten rule of surfing in cold water that, once you had put your wetsuit on, you had to get in. We had stood naked and barefoot in the car park and squeezed our shivering flesh into skintight full-length leotards made of damp and freezing six-millimetre-thick neoprene. Taking them off again without even having paddled out was unthinkable, even to me, and I was so terrified I was practically hyperventilating. I imagined that seals deprived of water felt like I did in my winter wetsuit. I would die of pure discomfort if I didn't get wet soon. I stuffed Blu-tack in my ears and pulled my hood up. The sea was at its coldest in February, between six and eight degrees.

Charlie went first. She waited for a lull and pushed off the rocks, paddling like crazy away from them. Watching her, my insides turned to liquid. Even if I managed to paddle out without getting smashed on the rocks, how on earth was I going to get back in? I allowed myself to glance down the beach, towards the bit I called Trauma Corner, where the undercurrent was so strong, it was easy to feel like you were nearly drowning, even on a calm day. The only part of the beach that still had sand on it was right down in front of the lifeguard hut, within easy sucking distance of Trauma Corner.

While I was dithering on the rocks, thinking about drowning, Charlie had made it out back, to the place of relative safety where the waves were no longer breaking. She stopped paddling and sat on her board, facing the horizon. There was a set coming. I could see it. My stomach clenched. Charlie paddled towards the first wave, as fast as she could. Then, instead of diving under it, she turned and tried to *catch it*. She looked over her shoulder at the looming mountain of water behind her, then she paddled with everything she had. She stood up, wobbling slightly because the surface of the wave was not smooth, but bumpy and uneven. Charlie rode the wave towards me, dived off just before she hit the rocks, then rode the current away from the rocks, took the rest of the set on the head, and made it out back again. I was sick with envy, speechless with admiration. She waved and beckoned, but I shook my head. I wasn't capable. I would die. Then I looked at the car park. I would die if I didn't get wet, too. Whatever I did, I was going to die. Charlie waved and beckoned again.

I thought about the *Tao-te-Ching*.

> *The highest good is like water.*
> *Water gives life to the ten thousand things and does not strive.*
> *It flows in places men reject and so is like the Tao.*[41]

This was nothing like I imagined the gentle-sounding *Tao* to be. But it was true that the highest good was water. I knew if I overcame my fear and paddled out into it, my tedious, mud-splattered, freezing, penniless, depths-of-winter existence would be transformed into something that felt meaningful. Surfing wasn't a sport or a disease, it was a religion. Hurling myself at the frothing ocean was a form of worship, an act of surrender. It put me in my place. It was holy. It made me feel whole.

I pushed off the rocks and paddled towards Charlie. There was an ocean of blood in my head, surging against my eardrums. I could hear my own heart beating. The water tasted of salt and fear, and the sky was dark and forbidding. I cleared

the rocks before the next set came – just – and then I was paddling for my life. Paddling for the horizon, paddling, paddling,
paddling, trying not to panic, trying to remember to breathe,
pushing the front of my board down with all my strength when
the first wave hit, feeling it ripped out of my hands, holding
my breath, scrabbling for the surface, drowning, drowning,
drowning. Then popping up, gasping, reeling in my board,
looking for the shore.

I sat on my board, beyond the place where the waves were
breaking – well beyond it – and watched the sky turn from grey
to orange to red. I didn't try to catch a wave. It was enough
to paddle out. The tide was pushing in. The lights of the pub
were beckoning us to safety. We paddled together down the
beach, towards the lifeguard hut. Charlie saw a little wave and
paddled towards it, caught it, scrambled to her feet, rode it
all the way to the beach. Home safe. I saw her struggle in the
shore break, then scramble out on to the sand, holding her
board high above her head.

I was all alone in the heaving ocean, under a darkening sky. I
could see a set gathering on the horizon, making curves where
straight lines should be. The sea was pitching all around me.
The sky was darkening so fast, I struggled to see the waves;
all I could see were glinting lines of white water. I turned my
board and paddled towards the shore. I didn't look behind me. I
waited until I felt the first wave catch me and drag me forward.
I stumbled to my feet, grabbed the side of my board, somehow
kept my balance in the middle of the foaming, swirling water.

I leaned into it, went with it, and, for one brief moment, all my terror disappeared. I was at the centre of the universe, in the still point of the turning world. Time was moving past me. I was alive.

'Woohoo!' Charlie said, when I joined her on the beach, beaming with the pleasure and relief of survival. 'Do you know what it's doing tomorrow?'

Spring

The true harvest of my daily life is somewhat
as intangible and indescribable as the tints of
morning and evening. It is a little star-dust caught,
a segment of the rainbow which I have clutched.

Winter went on forever, and then one day it was spring. I knew it was spring because I heard a skylark. I stopped in my tracks and searched the air, hoping to find it with my eyes. No luck. It was hiding in the sky. I gave up and carried on walking towards the west-facing beach, chased by the song of the skylark, until it was finally replaced by the sound of the sea.

The rocks were strewn with driftwood. I gathered the best pieces into a pile and stashed them at the bottom of the steps. I clambered over the boulders to the mouth of the cave and sat down, resting my chin on my knees, just like I had almost exactly a year ago, only then it had felt like winter and there was a storm coming in across the sea. The gannets were still diving, and the cave was still a cave, but the world looked altogether different. Thoreau was on Twitter. *Things don't change, we change*, he had tweeted that morning, from beyond the grave. But it wasn't true. The beach had changed completely. The boulders had been rearranged like garden furniture. The cairns were ancient history. Sand was heaped up in the mouth of the cave. The sea was flat, the sun was out. I turned my face to catch its warmth. I closed my eyes. I probably had more wrinkles than last year. I was time-worn, like the rocks. I had changed, and I had started to change the story I told myself about how I was supposed to live.

I sat for a long time, resting my face in the warmth of the sun, then I stood up and took off all my clothes and made my way over the boulders to the edge of the sea. I needed the tonic of wildness, as Thoreau put it. The ocean was the forest to my village: 'Our village life would stagnate if it were not for the unexplored forests and meadows which surround it.'[42]

The sea was still cold. I gasped my way in and out, then stood on a rock, like a cormorant, drying myself in the sun. I put my clothes on, then walked back towards the sea and climbed up the side of the cliff until I found a ledge to sit on where the flies couldn't reach me. All the water that had been in the river in Bristol that day, more than a year ago, would have been discharged into the sea by now. Maybe some of it had flowed in this direction. Maybe there was a droplet of my former life, right here, in front of my eyes, mixed in with all this change.

I thought about my old life sometimes, on dark days and during stormy nights when the wind was howling and the air was full of the sound of the sea smashing into the cliffs. I wondered what would have happened if I had stuck it out in the box room, given it time, waited for things to fall into place, instead of running away. I wondered if I had been too hasty.

I wondered about the forces that had carried me back to this place, with its ghosts and its faltering economy and its lack of ambition. The more I tried to make sense of things, the less sense they made. There were so many reasons why I did things. Half the time, the reasons were hidden, and the other half, they were in direct conflict with themselves.

I leaned back against the ancient rock, which the sun had already warmed up slightly, and I let my whole body relax. I could never relax when I lived in Bristol. I was always on edge, even in my room. Especially in my room. Maybe that was what I'd come back for: I wanted to be in the one place where the sounds and smells and flowers and trees and streets and paths were so familiar that every cell in my body could go quiet. I wanted to be where there was nothing to fight or flee from. I didn't want to be an exchangeable commodity. I wanted to put down roots. Almost all my schoolfriends who had made lives for themselves in other places had solid homes to come back to. No home equals no freedom. We need roots before we can grow wings.

The tide was out, exposing the soft-skinned creatures who lived in the rock pools. The lines of many colours in the rocks were like the flesh of the earth turned inside out. My heart turned inside out with the feeling of responsibility that seems to be a side effect of love. Edmund Gosse was already writing about the destruction of the coastline in Devon and Cornwall in 1907: 'The ring of living beauty drawn about our shores is a very thin and fragile one.'[43]

Did I love this place because I lived in it, or did I live in it because I loved it? I didn't know. I had to live in it, because it was where my shed was, and I had to live in my shed, because it was the only way I could do the things I needed to do, the only way I could afford to be myself, and make my contribution. Every life is a compromise, and we have next to no control over most of what happens to us. Especially the big things, like where we live and who our parents are and what kind of landscape looks and sounds and smells like home. We don't choose our flaws or our gifts. We don't set the limits of the universe, but we do have to live by them, as best we can.

Perhaps it didn't matter why I was there. What mattered was that I was somewhere, and that somewhere had significance for me. It was not any old place, it was *my* place. I had poured meaning into it, and therefore I loved it, and therefore I knew where to find the treasure, and I knew I would try to defend that treasure until the day I died. 'Only if you love something,' said Barbara Kingsolver, 'will you inconvenience yourself to work on its behalf.'[44]

I clambered down from my rocky perch and made my way back over the boulders to the wooden steps. I gathered up the little pile of driftwood I had collected and climbed the steps and walked back up the track towards the skylark. I walked fast. I was keen to get home. I wanted to carry on writing the second draft of my book about busking my way to the midnight sun, and from there to Portugal. I wanted to practise the songs I was about to start recording in a granite pig shed with the help of a new friend. I wanted to make a wood store out of the driftwood I had been collecting all winter. I wanted to see if the postman had delivered the books I ordered from Amazon. I wanted to play my new records. I wanted to get in my garden and prepare the ground and plant seeds so that I would have something to harvest in autumn. The Green Party recently suggested that we should measure wealth in terms of free time instead of money. By that measure, I was loaded. I spent my free time on the ongoing art project that was my life, and my spare time making the small amount of money I needed to survive.

I pulled my skateboard out of the hedge and built up some speed as I carved my way past the Monterey pines. I could smell the sap rising. The camellias that lined the lane were almost finished, their petals rotting into the ditch, making food for the worms. The sycamores were gaining leaves. The blackthorn was spilling its confetti. My tiny garden was full of forget-me-nots that had seeded themselves. The tiny blue flowers were like stars, the starlike eyes of the earth. There was a bird diving and swimming and cavorting in the sky. And there was another one, and another one, and another one, their forked tails glinting in the sunlight. The swallows were back.

Conclusion

I learned this, at least, by my experiment: that if one advances confidently in the direction of his dreams, and endeavors to live the life which he has imagined, he will meet with a success unexpected in common hours.

A lot has changed since I wrote these pages, or rather the bulk of them. I am tiptoeing towards respectability – who knows, by the time you read this, I might have made it over the line. I might have a wheelie bin and a council-tax code and a bottle of Chardonnay chilling in the fridge. Maybe this book has sold a million copies and I've bought the poet's field, planted trees all over it and established legal covenants for the barn owls and the sparrows. More likely, I will still be clinging on with my toenails, terrified of the postman, washing myself and my dishes in the same broken shower tray, trying to remember to rinse off the slugs, and worrying about how I'm going to pay for my MOT.

I finished my story about busking across Europe. It was published in the UK and the US, and was translated into Spanish, German, Chinese, Taiwanese and Korean. I like the idea that my story about busking from Norway to Portugal in my yellow Iveco, which I wrote in my shed on the far side of Land's End, has made it to all those countries, especially since I never have. I'm still skint, but it doesn't hurt like it used to. My shed is a buffer and a safety net. Basic needs can be satisfied very cheaply when you don't have a landlord to support.

My story made it over the crossroads, too, and into one of the cottages opposite the pond, where a retired farmer lived with his wife. One morning, they knocked on my door to tell me they had seen my book in the window of Waterstones in Truro. The farmer sparkled with something I later realized was pride.

'Dylan Thomas lived here once,' he said. 'Right here, on the crossroads. Must be something in the rain.'

I had never heard about Dylan Thomas coming to the peninsula, never mind living right here, on these crossroads, but, according to Google, it was true. He and Caitlin got married in Penzance register office in 1937, having lived together for six months in the same cottage the farmer and his wife lived in, which I had also lived in, for six months, when I was nine. He described the crossroads in a letter to Vernon Watkins, posted in 1936: 'We live here in a cottage in a field, with a garden full of ferrets and bees. Every time you go to the garden lavatory, you are in danger of being bitten or stung.'[45]

After the farmer's visit, I scratched a quote by Dylan Thomas into the soft wood of Dad's old drawing board, which I still use as my desk: 'I think that if I touched the earth it would crumble; it is so sad and beautiful, so tremulously like a dream.'[46]

Some of my neighbours have died, or moved into nursing homes. The free men who were building a hut out of pallets on land that didn't belong to them have been evicted, and the hut they built has burned down. The poet's field has been sprayed and sprayed again. Someone has driven a car on to it and left it there to rust. The fishermen have died and left their gardens to their sons, who show no sign (yet) of wanting to evict me. The people who have moved on to the crossroads since I arrived don't know (or don't care) that I'm illegal. They bring me cold beers, because they know I don't have a fridge. Even if I had the space, I wouldn't get a fridge. I've discovered it's easy to live without one, and that HFCs, the chemicals used in fridges and air conditioning, are up to nine thousand times more warming for the atmosphere than CO_2.[47]

One of my gardening clients read a piece I published online about living in the shed. Now, when I go to work for her, she puts the immersion heater on and clean towels on a heated towel rail and insists I take a long, hot shower when I finish working. Once, she bought me a winter coat. Twice, she's bought me shoes. It's human nature to be kind as well as greedy, and my client/friend knows, I think, that the culture of enterprise which enabled her to accumulate wealth and security has curdled into something much meaner and harsher and less fair. Andrew Hood, senior economist at the Institute for Fiscal Studies, knows it too: 'The wealth of younger generations looks set to depend more on who their parents are than was the case for older generations. Today's young adults will find it harder to accumulate wealth of their own than previous generations did, due to the sharp fall in home ownership.'[48]

I was born in the Winter of Discontent, a few months before Thatcher came to power. Between the end of World War Two and the year of my birth, the gap between rich and poor had been steadily narrowing. Since the year of my birth, it has been steadily widening.[49] The ideology behind Thatcher's policies was that markets would regulate themselves and wealth would trickle down. We know now that markets do not regulate themselves, and it's not wealth that trickles down, it's greed.

Housing is a major driver of inequality, and the housing crisis is a side-effect of greed, along with crises in ecology, mental health and happiness. According to a report published in 2015, the UK is the most unequal country in the EU.[50] Between 2000 and 2015, homelessness in the UK rose by forty percent. In November 2017, Shelter estimated that one in every two hundred people in Britain is homeless.[51] This epic homesickness is a symbol and a symptom of a wider cultural dispossession, and nobody is immune.

Instead of taking a good hard look at greed and its ugly consequences, successive governments have gone out of their way to make sure housing policy benefits the greedy, while depriving others of homes.

Right to Buy, the policy of selling off council houses at bargain prices, was introduced by Thatcher in 1980. The scheme was presented as a way to empower people who had previously been excluded from the property-owning classes. It was supposed to be a way for council tenants to take control of their own destiny. But, of the 1.5 million homes sold under Right to Buy, only a fraction have been replaced, and four in ten of the former council homes are not owned by former council tenants. They are owned by private landlords, who rent them out at twice the rate of social housing to people like Mum, who can't afford to pay.

Instead of social housing, there are private landlords like Charles Gow, who owns at least forty ex-council properties.[52] (His father, Ian Gow, was a Conservative minister and Thatcher aide during the peak years of the Right-to-Buy boom.) Since the mid-1990s, thanks to the lack of rent control in the UK, landlords like Charles Gow have made an average profit of 16.3 per cent on buy-to-let mortgages. Rents in London rose by 9 per cent in 2012 alone.[53] As George Monbiot put it, 'Landlords now possess the kind of power once wielded by Norman barons.'[54]

In 2015, the Conservative government introduced a policy called Help to Buy. Help to Buy, a system of government-backed loans for first-time buyers, was presented as a way to get more people on to the housing ladder and to encourage developers to build more houses. It didn't apply to the people who need homes the most, the millions with less than a hundred pounds in savings, because to apply for a loan you needed to have five per cent of the value of the house you wanted to buy – anywhere between £10,000 and £25,000. In fact, Help to Buy helped to make housing even more unaffordable by helping to keep house prices artificially high. The loans funnelled public money into the pockets of private developers, leaving the taxpayer with all the risk. Jeff Fairburn, the chief executive of

Persimmon, one of the house builders awarded public money in the form of Help to Buy contracts, recently awarded himself a bonus of £75 million (it was initially £100 million, but he agreed to reduce it). Even Conservative housing minister Dominic Raab seemed embarrassed by this blatant display of corporate greed.[55*]

Fairburn's bonus would have been enough to build well over a thousand good-quality, sustainable council houses, if you factored in the revenue each house would generate over five years.[56] Instead, public money is being squandered, and increasing numbers of vulnerable people are dying. Between 2013 and 2017, at least 230 homeless people died on Britain's streets. From 2017 to 2018, 440 homeless people died – almost twice as many, in a quarter of the time.

I'm all for building good-quality, sustainable council houses. But building more houses should be a last resort. New houses cost far more than even our inflated prices suggest, especially as most are not good quality or sustainable, but are built as cheaply as possible by private developers whose only motivation is short-term profit. Cement production is the second most polluting industry in the world, after oil. Land is rare and precious. The scraggy bits around the edges are where the wild things are.

According to the World Wildlife Fund's *Living Planet Report*

---

* Jeff Fairburn was asked to stand down as CEO of Persimmon in November 2018, amid continuing controversy over the size of his bonus and the profits from Help to Buy.

2018, sixty per cent of the world's wildlife has disappeared since I was born, just under forty years ago. This is a catastrophe, and not just for pandas.

> The nature conservation agenda is not only about securing the future of tigers, pandas, whales and all the amazing diversity of life we love and cherish on Earth. It's bigger than that. There cannot be a healthy, happy and prosperous future for people on a planet with a destabilized climate, depleted oceans and rivers, degraded land and empty forests, all stripped of biodiversity, the web of life that sustains us all.[57]

While the government gives private developers public money to build more houses, a million homes in the UK are empty (not even counting the sheds).[58]

There are nine thousand second homes in Cornwall alone. Six and a half thousand of them don't pay any council tax or business rates, because of something known as the 'seaside loophole'. This loophole (small-business rate relief, introduced by the coalition government in 2013) costs Cornwall Council £11 million a year, while the sudden influx of people in the holidays puts a huge burden on services.[59] And there are other ways second-home owners pay less tax. The initial cost of furnishing a second home can be claimed back against pre-tax profits, and the income gained from renting it out can be diverted into a pension. Across England as a whole, second homes are thought to be responsible for an £80 million shortfall in public finances.[60] Meanwhile, there continues to be no tax at all on the value of land.

The vast majority of people in the UK would benefit greatly from a tax on the value of land. As Danny Dorling points out, 'Few people own very large gardens, let alone grouse moors or office blocks. The land value tax would also revolutionise commercial property taxation. In one step, the nature of our relationship with land, property and housing would change.'[61] Council tax bills would fall as those who could afford to pay were forced to shoulder more of the cost of the services that add value to their property. Housing would be cheaper and more plentiful: 'A land tax means there is less economic sense in one family owning as many homes and as much land as possible, as it becomes more expensive to own more than you need.'[62]

In my sister's village, there has been plenty of house-building since I came to live in my shed. Some of it has been affordable, some most definitely has not. The affordable housing was built on a greenfield site at the top of the village, forming a kind of local ghetto, while, in the cove, some eighty per cent of the houses are second homes and holiday homes. According to the old model of putting the economy first, this makes sense. If we remember to ask ourselves what the economy is actually *for*, it would make a lot more sense to require people with spare houses to rent them out on long-term contracts to local people, for an amount that was fixed as a ratio of the average wage. Nobody would have to give up their home, only their *spare* home, and not for nothing, because rent would still be paid, only it would be a *fair* rent.

In contrast to taking food off supermarket shelves, or supplying energy, housing does not need to be stolen, only more equitably distributed. It can be made to belong to everyone just a little bit more than it currently does by extending rights, by saying that everyone has the right to be housed. Governments could transfer empty privately-owned property into social housing and those who are hoarding in a time of austerity could be cajoled, taxed or otherwise persuaded out of such behaviour.[63]

Home is fundamental, like teeth and feet and sleep and love. Home is a necessary part of the scaffolding that lets us get on with the business of living. For people who don't have houses, or secure, affordable tenancies, home *is* the business of living. This is a huge waste of talent and energy, and it makes us all poorer.

Tough times call for tough decisions, as successive governments are fond of telling us, before shifting the load on to those who are least able to carry it. Nine out of ten second-home owners are in the top half of the wealth distribution, often because they have benefited from a colossal rise in house prices. Whether by accident or design, they bet on housing and won big. It's a measure of how lost we are that even the most radical left-leaning Labour party in decades has only gone as far as saying we should double council tax on second homes and use the money to *build more houses*.

Economy and ecology are two sides of the same coin. Social justice depends on a healthy ecosystem. The poor will pay with their lives when countries shrink and flood and burn because of climate change. The poor will pay with their lives when the air becomes unbreathable. The poor will pay with their mental health when they lose even more access to nature. If we keep building houses that cost the earth, to protect the greedy from having to share, then our houses won't be worth the earth they're built on, because the planet will be uninhabitable. So-called wide-eyed, romantic love for the natural world, what Thoreau and his contemporaries would have called *Transcendentalism*, is more rational than the kind of economic fundamentalism that seems to want to sacrifice existence for money.

Danny Dorling begins his book about the housing crisis with a passage about freedom:

When we talk about housing and wealth, ultimately what we are talking about is our freedom. When a great disaster looms in housing so, potentially, does a disastrous loss of freedom.[64]

The irony of turning houses into money and reducing homes to casino chips is that it undermines everybody's freedom. It's not just the people at the bottom of the ladder who are exploited and enslaved, working stupid hours to pay off somebody else's mortgage. It's also the people halfway up, commuting stupid hours, doing jobs that ruin their bodies and their minds, keeping the walls of their houses white, because that's what the estate agents prefer, and half an eye on the market, because a crash would cost a lifetime of drudgery. And the people at the top, living in prisons of their own making, fortresses designed to keep the homeless and desperate out. Even kind and generous people with homes they cherish and have already paid for spend half their lives trying to justify their luck, tripping over rough sleepers, riddled with guilt, stricken with panic for their children, aware that the experience of being at home is becoming more and more exclusive every year.

The etymology of the word 'crisis' contains the root of opportunity – *the point at which change must come, for better or worse*. We can build more and bigger houses and keep them white and fill them up with gadgets, or we can get a life. We can be greedy for the things that are slowly killing life on earth, like expensive fridges and SUVs, or we can be greedy for the things that support life on earth, like soil and bees and trees. We can hunker down and fortify our houses, or we can widen our sense of home until it includes the whole earth and every creature living on it. This might be hopelessly naive. Or it might be the only chance we've got.

The closer I live to worms and birds and weather, the more I understand that the ocean my life sails on is a vanishing one, peopled with creatures whose numbers have halved every decade since I was born: sparrows and swallows, bees, butterflies, hedgehogs, dolphins, whales, sharks, seals. I want to take less from these creatures, because their existence is woven into the fabric of my life, and the more I take from them, the more I stand to lose. And the more I learn about this fragile, creaking home of mine, the more I understand that my shed is a fitter vessel for my voyage than an expensive room in an expensive house with oil-fired central heating and hot water that comes out of a tap. Just as an old wooden sailing boat is a fitter vessel for the lurching and sinking of a heavy sea than a tanker with a complicated engine and a dwindling supply of fuel.

The longer I sail in my shed, the harder it is to seriously entertain the thought of moving back into a house. Not just because it would mean sacrificing stories and songs on the altar of rent, but because houses and their contents seem tomb-like, places of hoarded dust and darkness, compared to the wealth of sea and sky and stars that nobody can ever own.

Some days, when the evening sun is lighting up my floorboards and my bones are full of the ocean and my skin is thick with salt, I even find a kind of peace. The peace of knowing that the true art of living is not to gather things and polish them and lay them out for others to admire, but to have next to nothing, get plenty out of it, and give the rest away.

Home

I close the borrowed laptop and stare out of the window again. It was morning when I started reading the old draft of my book in the boatbuilder's studio, and now it's evening. I can see a trawler making its way back to harbour. It's late, but still light. Nearly midsummer. The boatbuilder's garden is in shadow. The shed will be catching the last rays of sunlight. I wonder what's happening to the seeds I planted. My boyfriend bodged the broken door back together and put a new lock on it and I moved my cello to his place and that's it. I haven't been back. I can't face seeing the empty shelves and the lack of everything. Remembering the moment I entered the shed and found my possessions missing is like being punched in the stomach. Odd how thoughts and memories can have such consequences in the physical world.

There were notes on the laptop they stole, from a book called *Property and Personhood*, by an academic called Margaret Radin. I've lost the laptop and everything that was on it,

but I can still remember one particular quotation, word for
word:

> Memory is made of relationships with other people and the
> world of objects. Much of the property we unhesitatingly
> consider personal – for example, family albums, diaries,
> photographs, heirlooms, and the home – is connected with
> memory and the continuity of the self through memory.[65]

The shed represented continuity as much as freedom, I
realize now. It connected me to the past and the future and
provided a container for the objects that belonged to me.

'Belong' has its roots in 'relationship', from the Old English
Gelang, which means together with.

I try to think about my story and whether or not it's still true,
but I'm disorientated. The existence I describe in the manuscript
seems ringed with shadow now, like a village surrounded by
forest. I thought it was my job to hack the meaning out of life,
but what if there is no meaning apart from the one we invent?

I want to run away. Part of me wants to delete the manuscript
and all its flaws, reject the life it describes, forget about all the
lost revisions. I want to distance myself, call it naive, retreat into
cynicism, work to get on the right side of capitalism. I want to
stop caring about this place, or any place.

Another part of me knows I can't, because that would be
giving up, and giving up would be like dying. 'Who are we to
decide that it is hopeless?' wrote R. D. Laing.

The fight my manuscript tries to describe is nothing less than a fight for life, and the fight will be won or lost on the level of story. Every politician knows that what matters is who controls the narrative.

I turn the laptop back on and open Google Earth. Google Earth has not been updated for a while. As far as Google Earth is concerned, the shed is still in an advanced state of disrepair, abandoned, sad and lonely, just like it was when I first attempted to live in it. It's as if the past seven years never happened.

I close the borrowed laptop and start to gather up my things. I walk up the hill to the van and get in and turn on the engine. The music starts up by itself. It's my own music, songs I recorded with my boyfriend in the pig shed. They sound like they've been buried for fifty years and then dug up and transferred on to tape. It's how we wanted them to sound.

I'm homesick for the great unfinished emptiness
All those imaginary adventures that I can't forget.

We haven't finished the album. I feel a kick in the guts when I remember I haven't got a microphone or a sound card or a mixer anymore. God knows how long it'll take me to save up for another load of equipment.

They said it was too dark to be a wanderer
So I tried to squeeze my soul into their net.

I don't plan to turn off the A30 and on to the B-road that leads to my shed. I turn left out of pure habit and, once I've turned left, I decide I might as well carry on and take the next right, which cuts back to the A30, but I miss that too, and then I miss the next one, and then the only thing to do is turn around or go home.

> *And I hung on hard, because I long to be safe like you*
> *But I can't close my mind to be safe just yet.*

I can hear my phone ringing. I ignore it and let the little blue Berlingo find its way round the twists and turns in the road, which is narrower than usual because of all the flowers spilling out of the hedges. I pass the turning to the valley where I lived when I was seven, then I pass the turning to the house my parents built and lost, and then I'm on the long straight and the sun's in my eyes and I squint and there are the sparrows lined up on the roof, waiting for me.

I go into the garden first. The seeds I planted are doing okay, given that I haven't weeded the beds once. They're mostly not dead. I pick a tiny new leaf of spinach and nibble it like a rabbit while I wander round the familiar patch of ground, looking for things I planted, observing them like a mother. I start unwinding bindweed from the blackcurrant, gently, so as not to disturb the blossom. I chuck the bindweed in the fire pit, which is nearly obscured by the grass. I'll have to borrow Charlie's strimmer.

I unlock the door and go inside. I'm expecting total disorder, because that's what I left, but someone has tidied up. Charlie, or my boyfriend, or both of them. They're the only people who have keys. I'm winded with gratitude. The shed is full of space and light, instead of loss and chaos, and it smells the way it always has, of time and woodworm dust and instant coffee. I go out through the back door and stand on the decking made of pallets and scaffold planks. The sun is still high, but sinking.

I try not to think of them coming over the field, grabbing my pickaxe and smashing my door with it, wearing gloves. I try not to hate them. I force myself to feel sorry for them. The only reason anyone needs stuff that badly is because they're empty and don't have access to anything else, and because they think stuff will make them happy. I know that story.

My phone is ringing again. It's my sister. 'We set up a Just Giving page,' she says. 'We didn't want to tell you, in case you were embarrassed. We explained what had happened to your shed and stuff, and people gave money, mostly small amounts, but lots and lots of people gave. It's amazing.'

I can't speak.

'It's just so you can carry on with your life, get another laptop and maybe replace some of your records and other stuff.'

I still can't speak.

'Don't you want to know how much we raised?' my sister says.

After she tells me, I have to sit down on the edge of the bed. My chest is going up and down, and the adrenaline is turning into heat, and the heat is spreading through me like ink dropped into water.

I go back outside and stand on the pallets. The field is glowing. The air is warm and soft. The sun is in my eyes. The light is blinding. I'm in uncharted territory, baffled, humbled and bewildered, trying to process how much I have been given.

Afterword

In August 2019, Catrina was granted a Certificate of Lawfulness by Cornwall Council, meaning she can no longer be evicted from her shed. She received financial help from the Royal Literary Fund to cover backdated council tax, and is now a fully paid-up member of polite society, although she still doesn't own a fridge.

Acknowledgements

Thanks to my family – Daisy, Terry, Colin, Naomi, Kirstan, Rosie, Ben, Tristan, Tamsyn, Barney, Sasha, Joss – for ensuring there is never a dull moment, and coping with being written about. I love you all.

Thanks to JG, Andy & Tuppin, Jay, Marg, Eldrydd, John & Veronica, Hannah & Ralph, Kate, Sarah & Richard, Becky, Jane, Holly & Dave, Eunice, Paul & Nav, Colin & Deborah, Rebecca & Andrew, Chloe & Will – for letting me thaw out/wash/sleep/write/live in your houses (and gazebos).

Thanks to the Society of Authors – for much-needed financial support.

Thanks to everyone who gave to the JustGiving page, or just gave, after my shed was burgled. I have no words.

Thanks to all the boatbuilders – Dave Need, Jonty, Will, Chris, Andy. I am eternally grateful.

Thanks to Sarah & John – for keeping surfing affordable.

Thanks to my readers – Jay, Chloe, Naomi, Daisy – for making all the difference.

Thanks to my agent, Jessica Woollard, my editors, Rose Tomaszewska and Jon Riley, and the whole Riverrun team, for believing in this book, and working so hard to get it out into the world.

Thanks to Andy – for listening (and listening, and listening) and playing me all those beautiful records.

And finally, to Deborah – for guidance, encouragement, practical support, humour and uplifting conversation. Your spirit is in this book, and will be in all my others.

Sources

Thanks to the following books and their authors, for clearing the path and keeping the torches burning.

Gaston Bachelard, *The Poetics of Space*
John Berger, *Hold Everything Dear*
Wendell Berry, *The World-Ending Fire*
Annie Dillard, *Teaching a Stone to Talk*
Danny Dorling, *All that is Solid*
David Edwards, *Free to be Human*
Jay Griffiths, *Wild*
Clive Hamilton, *Growth Fetish*
Paul Kingsnorth, *Confessions of a Recovering Environmentalist*
Barbara Kingsolver, *Small Wonder*
Marion Shoard, *This Land is our Land*
E. F. Shumacher, *A Guide for the Perplexed*

Gary Snyder, *The Practice of the Wild*

Robert Sullivan, *The Thoreau you Don't Know*

Henry David Thoreau, *Walden*

Derek Wall, *Green History: A Reader in Environmental Literature, Philosophy and Politics*

End Notes

Homesick

1   Robert Sullivan, *The Thoreau You Don't Know: What the Prophet of Environmentalism Really Meant* (New York: HarperCollins, 2009), p. 48

Economy

2   UNHCR, at www.unhcr.org/uk/figures-at-a-glance.html

3   emmaus Bristol, at www.emmausbristol.org.uk/homelessness/homeless-in-Bristol

4   Joan Didion, 'Holy Water', in *The White Album* (New York: Simon & Schuster, 1979)

5   Jonathan Cribb, Andrew Hood and Jack Hoyle, 'The Decline

of Home Ownership Among Young Adults', at www.ifs.org.uk/publications/10505

6   Danny Dorling, *All That is Solid: The Great Housing Disaster* (London: Allen Lane, 2014), p. 169

7   Ibid. p. 296

8   Anna Minton, £100 Chickens: Anna Minton on House Price Inflation, at www.londonreviewbookshop.co.uk/blog/2017/7/100-chickens-anna-minton-on-house-price-inflation

Clothing

9   www.friendsoftheearth.uk/plastics/microfibres-plastic-in-our-clothes

10   Gerrard Winstanley, 'The True Levellers Standard Advanced: Or, The State of Community Opened, and Presented to the Sons of Men' (1649), at www.marxists.org/reference/archive/winstanley/1649/levellers-standard.htm

11   www.diggers2012.wordpress.com

12   www.labourland.org/benefits-of-land-value-tax

13   www.basicincome.org.uk/what_is_basic_income

14   Danny Dorling, *All That is Solid: The Great Housing Disaster* (London: Allen Lane, 2014) p. 93

Building the House

15   www.emoov.co.uk/reality-gap-uk-property-costs-eight-times-average-wage

16   Halifax Mortgage Calculator, at www.halifax.co.uk

Bread

17   www.beateatingdisorders.co.uk/media-centre/eating-disorder-statistics

18   Iain Pirie, 'The Political Economy of Bulimia Nervosa', in *New Political Economy*, Vol. 16 (No. 3), 2011, pp. 323–46

19   John Clare, 'The Mores' (1812–1831), at www.threeacresan-dacow.co.uk/2014/07/the-mores-by-john-clare

Architecture

20   Marcel Proust, *In Search of Lost Time 3: The Guermantes Way* (1920–21), translated by Mark Treharne (London: Allen Lane, 2002)

21   'Leader: Boris Johnson, a liar and a charlatan', *New Statesman*, 20 September 2017, at www.newstatesman.com/politics/uk/2017/09/leader-boris-johnson-liar-and-charlatan

22   Jim Waterson, 'Boris Johnson's Daily Telegraph salary revealed

to be £275,000', *Guardian*, 3 October 2018, at www.theguardian.com/politics/2018/oct/03/daily-telegraph-rehires-boris-johnson-on-275000-salary

Furniture

23   Alain de Botton, *The Architecture of Happiness*, (London: Hamish Hamilton, 2006), p. 59

Solitude

24   Gary Snyder, 'The Etiquette of Freedom', in his *The Practice of the Wild* (Berkeley: Counterpoint, 1990), p. 5

Philanthropy

25   Henry David Thoreau, *Walden; Or, Life in the Woods* (1854), (New York: Dover Thrift Editions, 1995), pp. 140-1
26   Ibid. p.154
27   Ibid. p.4
28   Naomi Klein, *No Logo*, (New York: Picador, 2000)
29   Henry David Thoreau, *Walden: Or, Life in the Woods* (1854), (New York: Dover Thrift Editions, 1995), p. 50
30   Wendell Berry, 'Why I Am Not Going to Buy a Computer', in

What Are People For? (Berkeley, California: Counterpoint, 1990), p. 177

31   Wendell Berry, 'God and Country', in *What Are People For?* (Berkeley, California: Counterpoint, 1990) p. 99

32   Kate Good, '4 Foods That Are Eating the World's Forests and How to Choose Better' (2017), at www.onegreenplanet.org/environment/foods-that-are-eating-the-worlds-forests-and-how-to-choose-better

33   John Vidal, '"Tsunami of data" could consume one fifth of global electricity by 2025' (11 December 2017), at www.climatechangenews.com/2017/12/11/tsunami-data-consume-one-fifth-global-electricity-2025/

34   Ian Sample, 'What is the Internet?' *Guardian*, 22 October 2018, at www.theguardian.com/technology/2018/oct/22/what-is-the-internet-13-key-questions-answered

Where I Lived and What I Lived For

35   Ty Bollinger, 'Understanding the Dangers of Glyphosate (& How to Minimize Exposure)' (2016), at www.thetruthaboutcancer.com/glyphosate-dangers

The Ponds

36   Jennifer Kennedy, 'Where Do Basking Sharks Go in the Winter?' (2 April 2018), at www.thoughtco.com/basking-sharks-in-winter-2291552

Visitors

37 Bernie Krause, *The Great Animal Orchestra* (London: Profile, 2013), p. 22

The Village

38 Henry David Thoreau, *Walden: Or, Life in the Woods* (1854) (New York: Dover Thrift Editions, 1995), p. 168

The Bean Field

39 BirdLife International, 'European Birds of Conservation Concern' (20 May 2017), at www.birdlife.org/europe-and-central-asia/European-birds-of-conservation-concern

Higher Laws

40 Robert Sullivan, *The Thoreau You Don't Know: What the Prophet of Environmentalism Really Meant* (New York: HarperCollins, 2009), pp. 151-2

The Pond in Winter

41   Lao Tsu, *Tao Te Ching* (6th century BC), (London: Wildwood House Ltd, 1973), verse 8

Spring

42   Henry David Thoreau, *Walden: Or, Life in the Woods* (1854) (New York: Dover Thrift Editions, 1995), p. 205

43   Edmund Gosse, *Father and Son* (1907), (London: Penguin, 1989)

44   Lidja Haas, 'Interview: Barbara Kingsolver', *Guardian*, 8 October 2018, at www.theguardian.com/books/2018/oct/08/barbara-kingsolver-fells-living-through-end-of-world

Conclusion

45   Dylan Thomas, from a letter to Vernon Watkins (April 1936), *Letters to Vernon Watkins* (London: Faber & Faber, 1957)

46   Dylan Thomas, 'Clown in the Moon' (1928)

47   Diego Arguedas Ortiz, 'Ten Simple Ways to Act on Climate Change' (5 November 2018), at www.bbc.com/future/story/20181102-what-can-i-do-about-climate-change

48   Rob Merrick, 'Inherited Wealth Will Decide How Rich Young People Will Become, a Study Warns', *Independent*, 5

January 2017, at www.independent.co.uk/news/uk/politics/
inherited-wealth-decides-rich-young-people-become-study-
bank-of-mum-and-dad-student-university-debt- a7509801

49   www.equalitytrust.org.uk/how-has-inequality-changed

50   Eurofound, *Recent developments in the distribution of wages in Europe*
(Luxembourg: Publications Office of the European Union,
2015), at www.eurofound.europa.eu/sites/default/files/ef_pub-
lication/field_ef_document/ef1510en.pdf

51   Shelter, 'More than 300,000 people in Britain homeless
today' (8 November 2017), at england.shelter.org.uk/media/
press_releases/articles/more_than_300,000_people_in_britain_
homeless_today

52   Nick Sommerlad, 'Great Tory Housing Shame: Third of
ex-council homes now owned by rich landlords', *Daily Mirror*,
5 March 2013, at www.mirror.co.uk/news/uk-news/right-to-
buy-housing-shame-third-ex-council-1743338

53   George Monbiot, 'The only way to fairness in housing is
to tax property' (2 June 2014) at www.theguardian.com/
commentisfree/2014/jun/02/housing-tax-property-help-to-
buy-government-schemes

54   Ibid.

55   Rob Davies, 'Persimmon chief's £75m bonus "almost unfath-
omable" – Raab', *Guardian*, 12 March 2018, at www.theguardian.
com/business/2018/mar/12/persimmon-chief-bonus-raab-
housing-help-to-buy

56   Gary Dunion, 'Here's how the Greens would build 500,000 council
houses' (25 February 2015), at bright-green.org/2015/02/25/how-
the-greens-would-build-500000-council-houses

57 WWF, *Living Planet Report 2018*, at wwf.panda.org/knowledge_
    hub/all_publications/living_planet_report_2018

58 www.emptyhomesuk.co.uk

59 Nosheen Iqbal, 'Are Holiday Homes Ruining the British Sea-
    side?', *Guardian*, 19 August 2018, at www.theguardian.com/
    money/2018/aug/19/are-holiday-homes-ruining-uk-seaside

60 John Ungoed-Thomas, 'Holiday homes dodge £80m council
    tax', *Sunday Times*, 29 July 2018, at www.thetimes.co.uk/article/
    holiday-homes-dodge-80m-council-tax-g39kv0xq7

61 Danny Dorling, *All That is Solid: The Great Housing Disaster*
    (London: Allen Lane, 2014), p. 220

62 Ibid. p. 75

63 Ibid. p. 267

64 Ibid. p. 1

Home

65 Margaret Jane Radin, 'Property and Personhood', *Stanford Law
    Review*, Vol. 34 (No. 5), May 1982, pp. 957–1015